Python Programming for Kids: Getting Started

Fun and Easy Guide to Building Your First Programs

Lily Anderson

Table of Contents

INTRODUCTION

Welcome to "Python Programming for Kids: Getting Started - Fun and Easy Guide to Building Your First Programs"! This book, written primarily for young readers eager to explore the intriguing world of coding, takes us on an exciting voyage into the world of computer programming using the Python language.

Python is not just any programming language; it's a great option for novices because of its readability and ease of use. This book is your key to learning Python programming in a fun and approachable way, whether you're a teacher searching for interesting resources, a parent hoping to introduce their child to the marvels of technology, or just a curious child.

We aim to empower young brains to design their software solutions by demystifying programming. We'll walk you through the foundations of Python programming, from comprehending basic syntax to creating your projects, using a combination of concise explanations, engaging examples, and enjoyable exercises.

You might question, though, why Python? Because of its simple syntax, which is similar to plain English, kids may easily understand and create code in Python. Furthermore, Python is a flexible language that finds application in various domains, including artificial intelligence, scientific research, web development, and game design. You're not just gaining a valuable skill by learning Python; you're also gaining access to countless opportunities in the digital age.

You're going to go on an imaginative and creative journey with this book. Each chapter offers engaging tasks to test your comprehension and spark your creativity, from printing messages and solving puzzles to creating games and interactive apps.

So, grab your computer, unleash your creativity, and join us as we embark on a thrilling journey through Python programming. Together, let's create some code to realize your concepts!

CHAPTER I

Getting Started with Python

What is Python?

Python is a high-level, interpreted programming language known for its simplicity and readability. Created by Guido van Rossum and first released in 1991, Python has since grown to become one of the most popular programming languages in the world, used by developers ranging from beginners to experts. The language's design philosophy emphasizes code readability and simplicity, making it an ideal choice for those new to programming and for those who value clear and maintainable code.

At its core, Python is a versatile and powerful language that supports multiple programming paradigms, including procedural, object-oriented, and functional programming. This flexibility allows developers to choose the best approach for their specific task. Python's syntax, which is deliberately designed to be easy to read and write, resembles plain English. This aspect not only lowers the barrier to entry for new programmers but also facilitates collaboration among teams, as all members easily understand the code.

One of the critical features of Python is its extensive standard library, often called "batteries included." This means that Python comes with a rich set of modules and packages that can be used to perform a wide range of tasks without requiring additional installations. These modules cover everything from file I/O, system calls, and web development to mathematics, data processing, and scientific computing. This extensive library support is one of the reasons why Python is a preferred choice for rapid application development and prototyping.

Python is also known for its strong community support. The Python Software Foundation (PSF) oversees the development of the language, ensuring its growth and maintenance. The community of Python developers is large and active, contributing to an ever-growing repository of third-party modules and packages available through the Python Package Index (PyPI). This ecosystem allows developers to extend Python's capabilities easily and share their own libraries with the world.

One of the reasons for Python's widespread adoption is its use in various fields and industries. Python frameworks such as Django and Flask are popular for building robust and scalable web applications in web development. Django, in particular, follows the "batteries included" philosophy, providing a range of built-in features for tasks like database interaction, form handling, and user authentication. On the other hand, Flask is a micro-framework that offers flexibility and simplicity, allowing developers to choose their own tools and libraries for different tasks.

Python has emerged as the language of choice in data science and machine learning. Libraries such as NumPy, pandas, and Matplotlib provide powerful data manipulation, analysis, and visualization tools. For machine learning, libraries like TensorFlow, Keras, and scikit-learn offer robust frameworks for building and training models. The integration of Python in these domains has been further bolstered by Jupyter Notebooks, which provide an interactive environment for writing and sharing code, visualizations, and narrative text.

Python's application extends to scientific computing and research as well. Libraries such as SciPy and SymPy cater to scientific and mathematical computations, while BioPython serves the bioinformatics community. Python's simplicity and readability make it a preferred language for researchers and scientists who need to write code for their experiments and data analysis without delving into the complexities of more verbose languages.

In the realm of automation and scripting, Python excels due to its ease of use and the powerful tools available in its standard library. System administrators and DevOps engineers use Python to automate repetitive tasks, manage infrastructure, and deploy applications. Tools like Ansible and SaltStack, which are written in Python, are widely used for configuration management and automation in IT environments.

Python's versatility is also evident in the field of education. Its straightforward syntax and readability make it an excellent language for teaching programming concepts. Many educational institutions and online platforms have adopted Python as the first language in their computer science curriculum. Tools like Turtle graphics make learning Python fun for kids, allowing them to create drawings and simple games while grasping fundamental programming concepts.

The language's use is not limited to these areas. Python is used for algorithmic trading, risk management, and quantitative analysis in finance. In gaming, libraries like Pygame enable the development of simple to moderately complex games. Python is even making strides in the field of artificial intelligence, with applications in natural language processing, computer vision, and robotics.

Python's design also prioritizes developer productivity and code maintainability. Its dynamic typing and automatic memory management simplify the development process by reducing the need for boilerplate code and memory management tasks. This allows developers to focus on solving problems and implementing features rather than dealing with the intricacies of the language.

One of the remarkable aspects of Python is its interoperability. Python can easily interface with other languages and technologies. For instance, Cython and ctypes allow the integration of C/C++ code, enabling performance optimization for critical code sections. Jython and IronPython facilitate the use of Python in Java and .NET environments, respectively. This interoperability makes Python a highly adaptable tool in diverse technological landscapes.

Despite its many advantages, Python is not without its limitations. One common criticism is its performance. As an interpreted language, Python is generally slower than compiled languages like C++ or Java. However, the development speed and ease of use for many applications outweigh the need for high performance. For scenarios requiring optimized performance, developers can use Cython or write performance-critical code in C/C++ and integrate it with Python.

Another limitation is Python's Global Interpreter Lock (GIL), which can be a bottleneck in multi-threaded applications. The GIL ensures that only one thread executes Python bytecode at a time, which can limit the performance of CPU-bound multi-threaded programs. However, this issue can often be mitigated by using multi-processing or integrating with other languages for parallel tasks.

The future of Python looks promising, with continuous improvements and an ever-growing community. Python 3.x, the current major version of the language, introduced several enhancements over Python 2.x, including better Unicode support, improved syntax, and more consistent standard libraries. The community's shift towards Python 3.x has solidified its position as the future of the language, with Python 2.x having reached its end of life in January 2020.

Python's simplicity, readability, and versatility make it a powerful tool for many applications. Its extensive standard library, strong community support, and growing ecosystem of third-party modules contribute to its appeal. Whether you are a beginner taking your first steps in programming, a scientist analyzing data, or a developer building complex applications, Python provides the tools and features necessary to get the job done efficiently and effectively. As technology continues to evolve, Python's role in shaping the future of software development and innovation is undeniable. Its influence spans across industries, driving advancements in web development, data science, artificial intelligence, automation, and beyond. In the educational sector, Python's approachable syntax and robust support for various paradigms make it an ideal choice for teaching fundamental programming concepts, inspiring the next generation of developers. As the Python community continues to grow and evolve, it is clear that Python will remain a cornerstone of modern programming, empowering users to solve problems, automate tasks, and create innovative solutions easily and elegantly.

Installing Python on Your Computer

Python is an accessible and versatile programming language that has gained immense popularity for its simplicity and readability. Before you can start harnessing the power of Python, you need to install it on your computer. This section provides a comprehensive guide to installing Python on various operating systems, including Windows, macOS, and Linux. Additionally, it covers essential post-installation steps such as verifying the installation, setting up an integrated development environment (IDE), and installing necessary packages.

To begin with, let's discuss installing Python on a Windows system. The process is straightforward and involves downloading the Python installer from the official Python website, which is python.org. Once you navigate to the website, you will find a "Downloads" section. Here, you should select the latest stable version of Python compatible with your Windows operating system. Choosing the Windows Installer (64-bit) is recommended if you are using a 64-bit version of Windows. After downloading the installer, run it to start the installation process. During installation, it is crucial to check the box that says "Add Python to PATH." This option ensures that Python can be accessed from the command line, which is necessary for running Python scripts and commands.

The installer will then present you with two options: "Install Now" and "Customize Installation." For most users, the "Install Now" option is sufficient, as it installs Python with the default settings, including the Python interpreter, IDLE (Integrated Development and Learning Environment), and pip (Python's package installer). However, if you want to customize the installation directory or select specific features, you can choose the

"Customize Installation" option. Once the installation is complete, you can verify it by opening the Command Prompt and typing "python --version" or "python -V." If the installation was successful, the command will display the installed version of Python.

Next, let's explore the process of installing Python on macOS. Like Windows, the first step is downloading the Python installer from the official Python website. On the website, navigate to the "Downloads" section and select the latest stable version compatible with macOS. Download the macOS installer package, which typically has a .pkg extension. After the download is complete, open the installer package to start the installation process. The installer will guide you through a series of steps, including agreeing to the license agreement and selecting the installation location. It is generally best to use the default settings unless you have specific requirements. Once the installation is complete, you can verify it by opening the Terminal application and typing "python3 --version" or "python3 -V." This command will display the installed version of Python, confirming that the installation was successful.

For Linux users, the process of installing Python can vary slightly depending on the distribution. However, most modern Linux distributions come with Python pre-installed. To check if Python is already installed, open a terminal and type "python3 --version" or "python3 -V." If Python is not installed or you need a different version, you can install it using the package manager for your specific distribution. For example, on Debian-based systems like Ubuntu, you can use the following commands to update the package list and install Python: "sudo apt update" followed by "sudo apt install python3." On Red Hat-based systems like Fedora, you can use "sudo dnf install python3." These commands will download and install the latest version of Python available in the repository. After the installation is complete, you can verify it by typing "python3 --version" or "python3 -V" in the terminal.

After installing Python, it is essential to ensure that the installation is correctly configured and ready for development. As mentioned earlier, one of the first steps is to verify the installation by checking the Python version. Additionally, you should check if pip, the Python package installer, is installed and working correctly. Pip is a powerful tool that allows you to install and manage additional Python packages and libraries. To check if pip is installed, open the command line (Command Prompt, Terminal, or shell) and type "pip --version." If pip is not installed, you can usually install it using the command "python -m ensurepip" or "python3 -m ensurepip" depending on your system's configuration.

Once Python and pip are installed and verified, the next step is to set up an Integrated Development Environment (IDE) to write and run your Python code. An IDE provides a user-friendly interface with features like syntax highlighting, code completion, debugging tools, and project management capabilities. Several popular IDEs are available for Python development, each with its unique features and advantages. Some of the most commonly used IDEs include PyCharm, Visual Studio Code, and IDLE.

PyCharm, developed by JetBrains, is a powerful and feature-rich IDE specifically designed for Python development. It offers advanced features like intelligent code completion, real-time code analysis, and a robust debugger. PyCharm is available in two editions: a free Community Edition and a paid Professional Edition. To install PyCharm, visit the JetBrains website, download the installer for your operating system, and follow the installation instructions. Once installed, you can create a new Python project and start writing code organized and efficiently.

Visual Studio Code (VS Code) is another popular IDE that supports Python development. Developed by Microsoft, VS Code is a lightweight and highly customizable code editor with many extensions. Download and install the editor from the official website to set up VS Code for Python development. After installation, open VS Code and install the Python extension from the Extensions Marketplace. The Python extension provides features like IntelliSense (code completion), debugging, and linting (code analysis). Once the extension is installed, you can create a new Python file and start coding.

IDLE, which stands for Integrated Development and Learning Environment, is a simple IDE that comes bundled with the Python installation. It is an excellent choice for beginners due to its simplicity and ease of use. To start IDLE, open your command line and type "idle" or "idle3" depending on your system's configuration. IDLE provides a basic editor and an interactive shell where you can write and execute Python code. While it may lack some advanced features found in other IDEs, it is more than sufficient for learning and writing small to medium-sized Python programs.

With Python installed and your development environment set up, you are ready to start writing and running Python code. However, as you progress, you may need to install additional packages and libraries to extend Python's functionality. This is where pip, the Python package installer, comes into play. Pip allows you to install packages from the Python Package Index (PyPI), a repository of over 200,000 Python projects. To install a package using pip, open your command line and use the command "pip install package_name," replacing "package_name" with the name of the package you want to install. For example, to install the popular NumPy library for numerical computing, you would use "pip install numpy." Pip will download and install the package, making it available for use in your Python projects.

In addition to pip, you may also encounter virtual environments, a tool that allows you to create isolated Python environments for different projects. Virtual environments are useful for managing dependencies and avoiding conflicts between packages. To create a virtual environment, open your command line and navigate to your project directory. Then, use the command "python -m venv env_name," replacing "env_name" with the name you want to give to your virtual environment. This command will create a new directory containing the isolated Python environment. To activate the virtual environment, use the command "source env_name/bin/activate" on macOS and Linux, or "env_name\Scripts\activate" on Windows. Once activated, any packages you install using pip will be contained within the virtual environment, ensuring that your project dependencies are managed separately from your system-wide Python installation.

Installing Python on your computer is the first step towards unlocking the power and versatility of this remarkable programming language. The installation process is straightforward and well-documented whether you are using Windows, macOS, or Linux. Following the steps outlined in this section can ensure a smooth installation and set up a robust development environment. With Python installed and configured, you can begin exploring the endless coding possibilities, from web development and data science to automation and artificial intelligence. As you continue to learn and grow as a programmer, you will find that Python's simplicity and readability make it an invaluable tool for bringing your ideas to life.

Running Your First Python Program

Learning to program can be a fun and rewarding experience, and Python is an excellent language for beginners due to its simplicity and readability. Running your first Python program is an exciting milestone on your programming journey. This section will guide you through the process, covering everything from understanding Python syntax and using different programming environments to writing and executing your first Python script.

To begin with, it's essential to understand what a Python program is. A Python program is a sequence of instructions written in the Python programming language that a computer can execute. These instructions can perform various tasks, from simple arithmetic operations to complex data processing. Python's syntax, which is the set of rules that define how a Python program is written, is designed to be intuitive and easy to understand, making it an ideal choice for newcomers to programming.

Before running your first Python program, you need to ensure that Python is installed on your computer. Python is available for various operating systems, including Windows, macOS, and Linux. You can download the latest version of Python from the official website, python.org. Once installed, Python has an interactive shell and a command-line interface, allowing you to run Python code interactively or execute scripts stored in files.

One of the simplest ways to run a Python program is through the Python interactive shell, also known as the Python REPL (Read-Eval-Print Loop). The interactive shell lets you type Python commands and immediately see the results. To start the Python interactive shell, open your command line (Command Prompt on Windows, Terminal on macOS, or your preferred terminal on Linux) and type "python" or "python3," depending on your installation. You should see a prompt indicating that you are in the Python environment. This prompt is usually represented by three greater-than signs (>>>).

In the interactive shell, you can instantly type simple Python commands and see the output. For example, typing print("Hello, world!") and pressing Enter will display the text "Hello, world!" on the screen. This simple program is often called the "Hello, World!" program and is traditionally the first program written by beginners when learning a new programming language. It demonstrates the basic syntax of Python and introduces the print() function, which is used to display output.

While the interactive shell is helpful for testing small snippets of code, most Python programs are written in text files called scripts. A Python script is a file containing a sequence of Python instructions, which can be executed as a whole. You need a text editor or an integrated development environment (IDE) to write a Python script. Some popular text editors include Sublime Text, Atom, and Visual Studio Code, while common IDEs for Python development include PyCharm, Thonny, and IDLE.

To write your first Python script, open your text editor or IDE and create a new file. Save the file with a .py extension, which indicates that it is a Python script. For instance, you can name your file "hello_world.py". In this file, type the following code:

print("Hello, world!")

This code is identical to what you typed in the interactive shell, but this time, it is stored in a file that can be executed multiple times. Save the file after typing the code. To run the script, open your command line and navigate to the directory where you saved the file. You can use the cd command to change directories. Once you are in the correct directory, type python hello_world.py or python3 hello_world.py, depending on your Python installation, and press Enter. You should see the output "Hello, world!" displayed on the screen, indicating that your script ran successfully.

Understanding the print() function is crucial as it is one of the fundamental building blocks of Python programming. The print() function takes one or more arguments and displays them as output. These arguments can be strings (text), numbers, or other data types. For example, print(42) will display the number 42, and print("The answer is", 42) will display "The answer is 42". The print() function can also format strings using techniques such as concatenation or formatted string literals (f-strings).

Another essential concept in Python programming is variables. Variables store data that can be referenced and manipulated throughout a program. To create a variable in Python, simply assign a value to a name using the equals sign (=). For example, message = "Hello, world!" assigns the string "Hello, world!" to the variable message. You can then use this variable in the print() function like this: print(message). Running this code will display "Hello, world!" just as before, but now the message is stored in a variable, allowing you to reuse and modify it as needed.

Python supports various data types, including integers, floating-point numbers, strings, lists, tuples, dictionaries, and more. Each data type serves a different purpose and offers specific methods and operations. For example, strings are sequences of characters and can be concatenated using the plus sign (+) or repeated utilizing the asterisk (*). Lists are ordered collections of items and can be indexed, sliced, and iterated over. Understanding these data types and their operations is crucial for writing effective Python programs.

Control structures are another fundamental aspect of Python programming. Control structures allow you to control the flow of execution in your program. The most common control structures are conditional statements and loops. Conditional statements, such as if, elif, and else, allow you to execute different code blocks based on certain conditions. For example:

```
number = 10
if number > 5:
    print("The number is greater than 5")
else:
    print("The number is not greater than 5")
```

This code checks if the variable number exceeds 5 and prints an appropriate message based on the condition.

Loops, such as for and while, allow you to execute a code block multiple times. A for loop iterates over a sequence of items, such as a list or a range of numbers. For example:

```
for i in range(5):
    print(i)
```

This code prints the numbers 0 through 4. The range() function generates a sequence of numbers, and the for loop iterates over this sequence, assigning each number to the variable i in each iteration. A while loop, on the other hand, continues to execute as long as a specified condition is true. For example:

```
count = 0
while count < 5:
    print(count)
    count += 1
```

This code also prints the numbers 0 through 4, but it uses a while loop that continues to execute as long as the count is less than 5. The += operator is used to increment the count value in each iteration.

Functions are another crucial component of Python programming. Functions allow you to encapsulate reusable blocks of code, making your programs more modular and easier to understand. To define a function in Python, use the def keyword followed by the function name and parentheses. For example:

```python
def greet(name):
    print("Hello, " + name + "!")
```

This code defines a function named greet that takes one argument, name, and prints a greeting message. To call the function, use its name followed by parentheses, passing any required arguments. For example:

```python
greet("Alice")
greet("Bob")
```

This code calls the greet function twice, passing different names as arguments. The function prints a personalized greeting message each time it is called.

Once you are comfortable with writing and running simple Python programs, you can explore more advanced topics and features of the language. For example, you can learn about file I/O (input/output) to read from and write to files, exception handling to manage errors gracefully, and object-oriented programming (OOP) to create and manage complex data structures. Python's extensive standard library and the vast ecosystem of third-party packages provide tools and resources for almost any task you can imagine.

To further enhance your Python skills, consider working on small projects and exercises that challenge you to apply what you have learned. Projects such as building a simple calculator, creating a to-do list application, or developing a basic game can be excellent ways to practice and reinforce your knowledge. Additionally, online platforms like Codecademy, Coursera, and LeetCode offer interactive tutorials and coding challenges to help you improve your programming skills.

Running your first Python program is essential to your journey as a programmer. By understanding Python syntax, using different programming environments, and writing and executing simple scripts, you can build a strong foundation for more advanced topics and projects. Python's simplicity, readability, and versatility make it an ideal language for beginners and experienced developers alike. As you continue to explore and learn, you will discover Python's immense power and potential, enabling you to create innovative solutions and bring your ideas to life.

Understanding Python Syntax

Python is a high-level programming language known for its simplicity and readability, making it a popular choice for both beginners and experienced developers. Understanding Python syntax is fundamental to writing efficient and effective Python code. This section will explore the core components of Python syntax, including variables, data types, operators, control structures, functions, classes, and modules, to provide a comprehensive understanding of how Python programs are structured and executed.

At the heart of Python syntax is the use of indentation to define the structure and flow of the program. Unlike many other programming languages that use braces or keywords to delimit blocks of code, Python relies on indentation levels. Each block of code, such as the body of a function, loop, or conditional statement, is indented by a consistent number of spaces or tabs. This indentation enforces readability and ensures the code's structure is visually clear. For example, an if statement in Python might look like this:

```python
if condition:

    # This is the body of the if statement
    do_something()
```

The indentation after the if statement indicates the block of code that belongs to it. Proper indentation is crucial because Python will raise an IndentationError if the indentation is inconsistent.

Variables in Python are used to store data that can be referenced and manipulated throughout a program. Python is a dynamically typed language, meaning that you do not need to declare the variable type explicitly. Instead, the type is inferred from the value assigned to it. For example:

```python
x = 10
name = "Alice"
is_valid = True
```

In this example, x is assigned an integer value, name is assigned a string, and is_valid is assigned a boolean value. Variable names in Python should be descriptive and follow the conventions of using lowercase letters and underscores to separate words (e.g., my_variable).

Python supports various data types, including integers, floating-point numbers, strings, lists, tuples, dictionaries, and sets. Each data type serves a specific purpose and comes with a set of operations and methods. Integers and floating-point numbers are used for numerical computations, while strings are used to represent text. Lists and tuples are ordered collections of items, with lists being mutable and tuples being immutable. Dictionaries are collections of key-value pairs, and sets are unordered collections of unique items.

Operators in Python are used to perform operations on variables and values. Python supports a range of operators, including arithmetic operators, comparison operators, logical operators, and bitwise operators. Arithmetic operators, such as +, -, *, and /, are used for basic mathematical operations. Comparison operators, such as ==, !=, >, and <, are used to compare values and return a boolean result. Logical operators, such as and, or, and not, are used to combine or negate boolean expressions. Bitwise operators, such as &, |, and ^, perform operations on the binary representations of integers.

Control structures in Python, such as conditional statements and loops, allow you to control the flow of execution in your program. Conditional statements, including if, elif, and else, enable you to execute different blocks of code based on certain conditions. For example:

```python
if x > 0:
    print("x is positive")
elif x == 0:
    print("x is zero")
else:
    print("x is negative")
```

In this example, the program checks the value of x and prints an appropriate message based on the condition.

Loops, such as for and while, allow you to execute a block of code multiple times. A for loop iterates over a sequence of items, such as a list or a range of numbers. For example:

```python
for i in range(5):
    print(i)
```

This code prints the numbers 0 through 4. The range() function generates a sequence of numbers, and the for loop iterates over this sequence, assigning each number to the variable i in each iteration. A while loop continues to execute as long as a specified condition is true. For example:

```python
count = 0
while count < 5:
    print(count)
    count += 1
```

This code also prints the numbers 0 through 4, but it uses a while loop that continues to execute as long as count is less than 5. The += operator is used to increment the value of count in each iteration.

Functions are essential components of Python programming that allow you to encapsulate reusable blocks of code. To define a function in Python, use the def keyword followed by the function name and parentheses. For example:

```python
def greet(name):
    print("Hello, " + name + "!")
```

This code defines a function named greet that takes one argument, name, and prints a greeting message. To call the function, use its name followed by parentheses, passing any required arguments. For example:

```python
greet("Alice")
greet("Bob")
```

This code calls the greet function twice, passing different names as arguments. The function prints a personalized greeting message each time it is called. Functions can also return values using the return statement. For example:

```python
def add(a, b):
  return a + b
```

This code defines a function named add that takes two arguments, a and b, and returns their sum. You can call the function and assign the result to a variable to use the returned value. For example:

```python
result = add(3, 5)
print(result)
```

This code calls the add function with the arguments 3 and 5, stores the result in the variable result, and prints the result, 8.

Classes are the foundation of object-oriented programming in Python. A class is a blueprint for creating objects, which are instances of the class. To define a class in Python, use the class keyword followed by the class name. For example:

```python
class Dog:

  def __init__(self, name, age):
    self.name = name
    self.age = age
  def bark(self):
    print(self.name + " says woof!")
```

This code defines a class named Dog with an initializer method (init) that sets the name and age attributes, and a method named bark that prints a message. To create an instance of the class, call the class name followed by parentheses, passing any required arguments. For example:

```python
my_dog = Dog("Buddy", 3)
my_dog.bark()
```

This code creates an instance of the Dog class with the name Buddy and age 3, and calls the bark method, which prints "Buddy says woof!".

Modules are a way to organize and reuse code in Python. A module is a file containing Python code that can be imported and used in other Python programs. To create a module, save your Python code in a file with a .py extension. For example, you can create a file named my_module.py with the following code:

```python
def greet(name):
    print("Hello, " + name + "!")
```

To use this module in another Python program, use the import statement. For example:

```python
import my_module
my_module.greet("Alice")
```

This code imports the my_module module and calls the greet function defined in the module, passing the argument "Alice". You can also import specific functions or variables from a module using the from ... import ... syntax. For example:

```python
from my_module import greet
greet("Bob")
```

This code imports only the greet function from the my_module module and calls it with the argument "Bob".

Understanding Python syntax is crucial for writing clear, efficient, and effective Python code. The core components of Python syntax, including variables, data types, operators, control structures, functions, classes, and modules, provide the building blocks for creating a wide range of applications. By mastering these components, you can develop your programming skills and harness the power of Python to solve complex problems, automate tasks, and create innovative solutions. Python's simplicity and readability, combined with its extensive standard library and active community, make it an ideal language for both beginners and experienced developers. As you continue to explore and learn Python, you will discover its versatility and potential, enabling you to bring your ideas to life and make meaningful contributions to the world of technology.

CHAPTER II

Basic Python Concepts

Printing Messages

Printing messages to the screen is one of the most fundamental and frequently used operations in any programming language, and Python is no exception. The ability to display information to the user is crucial for debugging, user interaction, and providing feedback. In Python, the print() function is the primary tool for this task. This section explores the various aspects of printing messages in Python, including basic usage, formatting options, handling different data types, and advanced techniques.

At its core, Python's print() function is simple to use. You can display that string on the screen by calling print() with a string argument. For example, print("Hello, world!") outputs the text "Hello, world!" to the console. This simplicity makes print() an ideal starting point for beginners learning Python, as it provides immediate feedback and helps in understanding how code execution works.

The print() function is versatile and can handle multiple arguments. When multiple items are passed to print(), they are separated by a space by default. For example, print("Hello,", "world!") prints "Hello, world!" The function can accept any number of arguments, allowing you to print multiple pieces of information in a single call. This feature is helpful for debugging, as it lets you inspect the values of various variables at once.

Python's print() function is not limited to strings; it can also handle various data types, including integers, floats, lists, and dictionaries. When a non-string argument is passed to print(), Python automatically converts it to a string using the str() function. For example, print(42) prints the number 42, and print(3.14) prints the floating-point number 3.14. This automatic type conversion makes print() a powerful tool for inspecting variables and understanding program behavior.

One of the critical features of the print() function is its ability to format output. Python provides several ways to format strings, each offering different levels of control and flexibility. The simplest method is string concatenation, combining strings using the + operator. For example, print("The answer is " + str(42)) prints "The answer is 42". However, this approach can be cumbersome and error-prone, especially when dealing with multiple variables or complex data.

A more powerful and flexible way to format strings is using the format() method. The format() method allows you to insert variables into a string by using placeholders marked by curly braces ({}). For example, print("The answer is {}".format(42)) prints "The answer is 42". You can include multiple placeholders in a string and pass the corresponding values as arguments to format(). For example, print("{} + {} = {}".format(2, 3, 2 + 3)) prints "2 + 3 = 5". The format() method also supports named placeholders and various formatting options, such as specifying the number of decimal places or padding numbers with zeros.

In Python 3.6 and later, formatted string literals, also known as f-strings, provide an even more concise and readable way to format strings. F-strings are prefixed with an f or F, allowing you to embed expressions directly within curly braces. For example, answer = 42; print(f"The answer is {answer}") prints "The answer is

42". F-strings support all the formatting options available in the format() method and can evaluate arbitrary expressions, making them a powerful tool for creating dynamic and well-formatted output.

The print() function offers several optional parameters that give you additional control over how output is displayed. The sep parameter specifies the separator between multiple arguments, which defaults to a space. For example, print("Hello", "world", sep=", ") prints "Hello, world". The end parameter specifies what to print at the end of the output, which defaults to a newline character (\n). For example, print("Hello", end="! ") prints "Hello! " without moving to a new line, allowing subsequent print() calls to continue on the same line. These parameters can be used together to create custom output formats tailored to your needs.

In addition to standard output, Python's print() function can be directed to write to files. Using the file parameter, you can specify a file object where the output should be written instead of the console. For example, with open("output.txt", "w") as file: print("Hello, world!", file=file) writes "Hello, world!" to a file named output.txt. This feature is helpful for logging program output, saving results, or generating reports.

Python also provides advanced techniques for printing messages, such as using the sys module to control output more precisely. The sys.stdout object represents the standard output stream, which you can use to print messages directly. For example, import sys; sys.stdout.write("Hello, world!\n") prints "Hello, world!" to the console. This approach offers more control over output formatting and can be helpful in situations where print() does not provide the desired behavior.

Another advanced technique involves creating custom print functions to handle specific output requirements. You can add additional logic or formatting rules by defining your own function that wraps the print() function. For example, you might create a custom print function that automatically prefixes messages with a timestamp or log level. Custom print functions can help standardize output across a program and make it easier to implement consistent logging and debugging practices.

Understanding the nuances of the print() function and its various features is essential for effective programming in Python. Printing messages is not just about displaying information; it is a critical tool for debugging, testing, and interacting with users. By mastering the different ways to format and control output, you can create more readable and informative programs that are easier to develop, maintain, and debug.

In addition to its role in debugging and user interaction, the print() function plays a vital role in teaching and learning Python. For beginners, seeing immediate feedback from their code helps reinforce concepts and build confidence. The simplicity of print() makes it an accessible starting point for exploring more complex programming constructs, such as loops, conditionals, and functions. As learners progress, they can use print() to visualize the behavior of algorithms, inspect data structures, and understand the execution flow.

In professional software development, effective use of print() and other output techniques can improve the quality and maintainability of code. Clear and well-formatted output makes it easier to trace the execution of a program, identify bugs, and understand the impact of changes. Print statements are often combined with logging libraries to provide comprehensive and configurable logging capabilities. Python's built-in logging module offers a flexible framework for generating log messages with different severity levels, output destinations, and formatting options.

The print() function is crucial in creating interactive applications and command-line tools. By printing prompts and messages to the console, programs can guide users through input processes, provide feedback, and display results. Interactive applications often rely on a combination of print() for output and input() for user input, creating a dynamic and responsive user experience. Understanding how to use print() effectively in these contexts is crucial in building intuitive and user-friendly interfaces.

Furthermore, printing messages is essential for communicating with other developers and stakeholders. Clear and concise output can help convey the purpose and behavior of code, making it easier to collaborate on projects, review code, and share results. In scientific computing, data analysis, and research, generating well-formatted output is crucial for documenting findings, creating visualizations, and presenting results.

In conclusion, the print() function is a fundamental and versatile tool in Python programming. From primary usage and formatting options to advanced techniques and professional applications, understanding how to print messages effectively is essential for success in Python. By mastering the various features and capabilities of print(), you can create clear, informative, and user-friendly output that enhances your programs and facilitates development, debugging, and communication. Whether you are a beginner learning the basics or an experienced developer working on complex projects, the ability to print messages in Python is a valuable skill that will serve you well throughout your programming journey.

Using Variables

Variables are fundamental to programming in Python and most other programming languages. They act as storage containers for data that can be referenced and manipulated throughout a program. Understanding how to use variables effectively is crucial for writing precise, efficient, and maintainable code. This section delves into the concept of variables, exploring their types, scope, naming conventions, and best practices in Python.

At its core, a variable is a symbolic name associated with a value and whose associated value may be changed. Variables enable programmers to store data, which can then be used and manipulated within the program. In Python, variables are dynamically typed, meaning you do not need to declare their type explicitly. Instead, the type is inferred from the value assigned to the variable. This feature makes Python a flexible and user-friendly language, especially for beginners.

To create a variable in Python, you simply use an assignment statement consisting of a variable name, an equals sign (=), and the value you want to assign to the variable. For example, the statement x = 10 assigns the integer value 10 to the variable x. Once a variable is created, its value can be accessed and modified. For instance, you can later change the value of x by assigning a new value, such as x = 20. This reassignment updates the value stored in the variable, allowing you to reuse variable names without causing conflicts.

Python supports various data types that can be stored in variables, including integers, floating-point numbers, strings, lists, tuples, dictionaries, and sets. Each data type serves a different purpose and offers specific methods and operations. For example, integers and floating-point numbers are used for numerical computations, while strings are used to represent text. Lists and tuples are ordered collections of items, with lists being mutable (modifiable) and tuples being immutable (non-modifiable). Dictionaries are collections of key-value pairs, and sets are unordered collections of unique items.

The ability to store different data types in variables and manipulate them is a powerful feature of Python.

Naming variables is an essential aspect of writing readable and maintainable code. Variable names should be descriptive and follow a consistent naming convention. In Python, variable names are case-sensitive and can include letters, digits, and underscores, but they must start with a letter or an underscore. For example, my_variable and myVariable are valid variable names, but 2variable is not. The convention for variable names in Python is to use lowercase letters and underscores to separate words, known as snake_case. For instance, total_cost, user_name, and file_path are examples of well-named variables. Adhering to naming conventions makes your code easier to read and understand for yourself and others who may work with your code.

The scope of a variable refers to the region of a program where the variable is accessible. In Python, variables can have different scopes depending on where they are defined. The two main types of scope are local and global. A variable defined inside a function has a local scope and is only accessible within that function. For example:

```
def my_function():
  local_variable = 10
  print(local_variable)


my_function()

print(local_variable)  # This will cause an error because
local_variable is not defined outside the function
```

In this example, local_variable is defined inside my_function() and can only be accessed within that function. Trying to access local_variable outside the function results in an error. Conversely, a variable defined outside any function has a global scope and is accessible throughout the entire program. For example:

```
global_variable = 20

def my_function():
  print(global_variable)

my_function()
print(global_variable)
```

In this example, global_variable is defined outside any function and can be accessed inside and outside my_function(). It is essential to understand variable scope to avoid unintended behaviors and bugs in your programs.

Sometimes, you may need to modify a global variable inside a function. To do this, you use the global keyword to declare that you are referring to the global variable, not a local one. For example:

```
global_variable = 30

def modify_global():
  global global_variable
  global_variable = 40

modify_global()
print(global_variable) # This will print 40
```

In this example, the global keyword allows the function modify_global() to modify the value of global_variable. Without the global keyword, global_variable inside the function would be treated as a local variable, and the modification would not affect the global variable.

Another essential concept in Python is variable lifetime, which refers to the duration for which a variable exists in memory. Variables with global scope exist for the duration of the program, while variables with local scope exist only for the duration of the function in which they are defined. When a function finishes execution, its local variables are destroyed, and their memory is reclaimed by the system. Understanding variable lifetime helps manage memory usage and avoid memory leaks in your programs.

In addition to basic variables, Python supports advanced features like mutable and immutable objects. Mutable objects, such as lists and dictionaries, can be modified after creation. For example, you can add, remove, or change items in a list. Immutable objects, such as strings and tuples, cannot be modified after they are created. Any attempt to change an immutable object creates a new object. For example:

immutable_string = "hello"

new_string = immutable_string + " world"

print(new_string) # This will print "hello world"

In this example, concatenating " world" to immutable_string creates a new string, new_string, without modifying the original immutable_string.

Understanding the difference between mutable and immutable objects is crucial for writing efficient and bug-free code. For instance, when passing mutable objects to functions, changes made to the object inside the function will affect the original object. However, changes to immutable objects result in new objects being created. For example:

```python
def modify_list(my_list):
  my_list.append(4)

my_list = [1, 2, 3]

modify_list(my_list)

print(my_list) # This will print [1, 2, 3, 4]

def modify_string(my_string):

  my_string += " world"

my_string = "hello"

modify_string(my_string)

print(my_string) # This will print "hello"
```

In this example, modifying my_list inside modify_list() affects the original list because lists are mutable. However, modifying my_string inside modify_string() does not affect the original string because strings are immutable.

Python also supports multiple assignment, allowing you to assign values to multiple variables in a single statement. For example:

```python
a, b, c = 1, 2, 3

print(a) # This will print 1

print(b) # This will print 2
```

```python
print(c) # This will print 3
```

This feature is useful for swapping values between variables or unpacking values from a collection. For example, you can swap the values of two variables without using a temporary variable:

```python
x = 5
y = 10
x, y = y, x
print(x) # This will print 10
print(y) # This will print 5
```

In addition to basic assignment, Python allows variable unpacking from lists, tuples, and other iterable objects. For example:

```python
my_tuple = (4, 5, 6)
a, b, c = my_tuple
print(a) # This will print 4
print(b) # This will print 5
print(c) # This will print 6
```

This feature simplifies code and makes it more readable, especially when working with functions that return multiple values.

Best practices for using variables in Python include choosing meaningful variable names, following naming conventions, and keeping variable scope limited to where it is needed. Descriptive variable names make your code more readable and easier to understand. For example, total_price is more informative than tp. Following naming conventions, such as using snake_case for variable names, ensures consistency and readability. Keeping variable scope limited to where it is needed helps prevent unintended interactions and bugs. For example, avoid using global variables unless necessary, and prefer local variables for temporary data within functions.

In conclusion, variables are a fundamental aspect of Python programming, enabling the storage and manipulation of data. Understanding how to use variables effectively involves knowing their types, scope, naming conventions, and lifetime. You can write clear, efficient, and maintainable code by mastering these concepts. Variables in Python provide the flexibility to work with different data types and support advanced features like multiple assignment and unpacking. Adhering to best practices for variable usage helps ensure your code is readable, consistent, and bugs-free. Whether you are a beginner learning the basics or an experienced developer working on complex projects, understanding variables is essential for successful programming in Python.

Basic Arithmetic Operations

Arithmetic operations form the foundation of numerical computation in any programming language, and Python is no exception. Understanding and using basic arithmetic operations is crucial for solving many problems, from simple calculations to complex algorithms. This section explores the fundamental arithmetic operations in Python, including addition, subtraction, multiplication, division, and more advanced operations such as modulus, exponentiation, and floor division. Additionally, it covers handling different numeric types, operator precedence, and practical applications of arithmetic operations in programming.

In Python, arithmetic operations are performed using standard operators. The addition operator (+) is used to add two numbers. For example, the expression 5 + 3 evaluates to 8. Addition can be used with integers, floating-point numbers, and even complex numbers. The subtraction operator (-) subtracts one number from another, such as 10 - 4, which evaluates to 6. Like addition, subtraction works with various numeric types. These operations are straightforward and form the basis for more complex mathematical expressions.

Multiplication in Python is performed using the asterisk (*) operator. For instance, 7 * 6 results in 42. Multiplication can be applied to integers, floating-point numbers, and complex numbers. One exciting aspect of the multiplication operator is its use with strings. In Python, multiplying a string by an integer repeats the string that many times. For example, "hello" * 3 produces "hellohellohello". This feature can be helpful for generating repeated patterns or formatting output.

The division is carried out using the forward-slash (/) operator. The expression 15 / 3 evaluates to 5.0, and 10 / 4 results in 2.5. In Python 3, the division operator always returns a floating-point number, even if the operands are both integers. This behavior ensures that division operations provide precise results and avoid truncating decimal points. Python provides the floor division operator (//) for situations where integer division is needed. The expression 10 // 3 evaluates to 3, discarding the remainder and providing an integer result. Floor division is helpful in scenarios where whole numbers are required, such as calculating the number of complete groups in a dataset.

The modulus operator (%) returns the remainder of a division operation. For example, 10 % 3 evaluates to 1 because 10 divided by 3 leaves a remainder of 1. The modulus operator is particularly useful in various applications, such as determining whether a number is even or odd. For instance, num % 2 evaluates to 0 if num is even and 1 if num is odd. Modulus operations are also employed in algorithms that involve cyclical patterns, such as circular buffers or repeating sequences.

Exponentiation in Python is performed using the double asterisk (**) operator. The expression 2 ** 3 evaluates to 8, as it calculates 2 raised to the power of 3. Exponentiation is essential in various fields, including scientific computing, engineering, and finance, where exponential growth or decay is modeled. Python's support for exponentiation with both integers and floating-point numbers allows for precise and efficient calculations in these domains.

Operator precedence determines the order in which operations are evaluated in an expression. In Python, operations follow the standard mathematical precedence rules. For example, multiplication and division have higher precedence than addition and subtraction. Therefore, the expression 2 + 3 * 4 evaluates to 14, not 20, because the multiplication is performed before the addition. Parentheses can be used to override the default precedence and specify the desired order of operations. For instance, (2 + 3) * 4 evaluates to 20, as the addition is performed first. Understanding operator precedence is crucial for writing correct and predictable code, especially in complex expressions.

Python supports various numeric types, including integers, floating-point numbers, and complex numbers. Integers are whole numbers without a decimal point, while floating-point numbers contain a decimal point and can represent fractional values. Complex numbers consist of a real and imaginary parts, represented as a + bj, where a is the real part and b is the imaginary part. Arithmetic operations can be performed on these numeric types, and Python handles type conversion automatically when necessary. For example, adding an integer to a floating-point number results in a floating-point number, as in 5 + 3.2, which evaluates to 8.2.

Python provides various functions and modules to enhance arithmetic operations. The math module offers various mathematical functions, such as square root, logarithms, and trigonometric functions. For example, math.sqrt(16) returns 4.0, the square root of 16, and math.log(10) returns the natural logarithm of 10. These functions extend the capabilities of basic arithmetic operations and enable more advanced mathematical computations.

In addition to the math module, Python's standard library includes the decimal and fractions modules, which support high-precision arithmetic and rational number computations, respectively. The decimal module is beneficial in financial applications where precise decimal representation is crucial. For instance, decimal.Decimal('0.1') + decimal.Decimal('0.2') evaluates to Decimal('0.3'), avoiding the floating-point inaccuracies that can occur with binary floating-point representation. The fractions module allows for exact arithmetic with rational numbers. For example, fractions.Fraction(1, 3) + fractions.Fraction(1, 6) evaluates to Fraction(1, 2), accurately representing the result.

Arithmetic operations are fundamental in mathematical calculations and play a vital role in various programming tasks. For example, loops and conditionals often rely on arithmetic operations to control the execution flow. In a for loop, the loop counter is typically incremented or decremented using arithmetic operations. For instance, the loop for i in range(5): print(i) prints the numbers 0 through 4 by incrementing i in each iteration. Similarly, arithmetic operations are used in conditional statements to compare values and make decisions based on the results. For example, if x > 10: print("x is greater than 10") evaluates the condition and prints the message if x is greater than 10.

Arithmetic operations are also essential in algorithms and data structures. Sorting algorithms like quicksort and mergesort rely on arithmetic operations to compare and swap elements. Search algorithms, such as binary search, use arithmetic operations to calculate the middle index of a list and narrow down the search range. Data structures like arrays, linked lists, and trees often involve arithmetic operations to traverse and manipulate elements. For example, accessing an element in an array involves calculating its index using arithmetic operations.

In computer graphics, arithmetic operations are used to transform and manipulate shapes, colors, and images. Scaling, rotating, and translating objects in a 2D or 3D space involve arithmetic operations on coordinates and vectors. Color manipulation, such as blending and filtering, requires arithmetic operations on color values. Image processing techniques, such as convolution and edge detection, rely on arithmetic operations to apply filters and detect patterns in pixel data.

Arithmetic operations are used to model and simulate physical systems in scientific computing and engineering. Numerical methods, such as finite difference and finite element methods, involve arithmetic operations to approximate solutions to differential equations. Signal processing techniques, such as Fourier transform and digital filtering, rely on arithmetic operations to analyze and manipulate signals. Control systems, such as PID controllers, use arithmetic operations to calculate control signals based on error values and system parameters.

Arithmetic operations are used in finance to calculate interest, investment returns, and financial metrics. Compound interest, for example, involves exponentiation to calculate the growth of an investment over time. Present value and future value calculations use arithmetic operations to determine the value of cash flows at different points in time. Financial ratios, such as price-to-earnings and debt-to-equity ratios, involve arithmetic operations to analyze a company's financial health.

In data analysis and machine learning, arithmetic operations are used to preprocess and analyze data. Descriptive statistics, such as mean, median, and standard deviation, involve arithmetic operations to summarize data. Data normalization and scaling, which are essential steps in machine learning, use arithmetic operations to transform data into a consistent range. Gradient descent, a standard optimization algorithm in machine learning, relies on arithmetic operations to update model parameters iteratively.

In everyday applications, arithmetic operations are used to perform calculations in spreadsheets, generate invoices, and manage budgets. Spreadsheet software, such as Microsoft Excel and Google Sheets, uses arithmetic operations to perform calculations on cell values. Formulas and functions like SUM, AVERAGE, and IF involve arithmetic operations to analyze and manipulate data. Invoices and budgets use arithmetic operations to calculate totals, taxes, and discounts.

In conclusion, basic arithmetic operations are a cornerstone of programming in Python and play a crucial role in many applications. Understanding and using addition, subtraction, multiplication, division, modulus, exponentiation, and floor division are essential for solving mathematical problems and implementing algorithms. Python's support for various numeric types, operator precedence, and advanced mathematical functions enhances its capabilities for arithmetic operations. By mastering these operations, programmers can tackle complex computational tasks, model physical systems, analyze data, and create innovative solutions across diverse domains. Whether in scientific computing, finance, data analysis, or everyday applications, arithmetic operations are fundamental tools that enable precise and efficient problem-solving in Python.

Getting User Input

User input is crucial to many software applications, allowing programs to interact dynamically with users. In Python, capturing user input is straightforward, thanks to its built-in functions and user-friendly syntax. This section explores the mechanisms for getting user input in Python, covering basic input methods, data validation, handling different data types, and advanced techniques such as command-line arguments and graphical user interfaces.

The primary function for capturing user input in Python is input(). This function reads a line from the user input (usually from the keyboard) and returns it as a string. The basic usage of input() involves prompting the user with a message and waiting for their response. For example, name = input("Enter your name: ") prompts the user to enter their name and stores the input in the variable name. The input() function is versatile and can be used to capture various types of data, although it always returns the input as a string.

Handling user input effectively often requires converting the input from a string to another data type, such as an integer or a float. This conversion is necessary because the input() function always returns a string, even when the user enters numeric data. For instance, to get an integer input from the user, you can use age = int(input("Enter your age: ")). Here, the int() function converts the string returned by input() into an integer. Similarly, to capture a floating-point number, you use weight = float(input("Enter your weight: ")). These conversions are essential for performing arithmetic operations or comparisons on the user-provided data.

Data validation is critical to handling user input to ensure that the input is appropriate and meaningful for the application. In Python, data validation involves checking the input against certain criteria and providing feedback if the input does not meet the expectations. For example, to validate that the user has entered a positive integer, you might use a while loop to repeatedly prompt the user until they provide valid input:

```python
while True:

    try:

        age = int(input("Enter your age: "))

        if age > 0:
```

```python
        break

    else:

        print("Please enter a positive integer.")

    except ValueError:

    print("Invalid input. Please enter an integer.")
```

In this example, the loop continues to prompt the user until they enter a valid positive integer. The try block attempts to convert the input to an integer, and the except block catches any ValueError exceptions that occur if the input is not a valid integer. This approach ensures that the program only proceeds with valid input, enhancing its robustness and reliability.

Handling different types of user input often requires specific validation techniques. For instance, you might use the datetime module to parse and validate the input when capturing a date. Here's an example of how to validate a date input:

```python
from datetime import datetime

while True:

    date_str = input("Enter a date (YYYY-MM-DD): ")

    try:

date = datetime.strptime(date_str, "%Y-%m-%d")

        break

    except ValueError:

        print("Invalid date format. Please enter the date in YYYY-MM-DD format.")
```

In this example, the datetime.strptime() function is used to parse the input string according to the specified format. If the input does not match the format, a ValueError is raised, prompting the user to try again. This method ensures that the input is a valid date, which can then be used for further processing.

Python also allows for more advanced user input techniques, such as capturing command-line arguments. Command-line arguments enable users to provide input to a program when it is executed, rather than interactively during its run. This approach is common in scripts and utilities that need to process files, configure options, or run batch operations. The sys module provides access to command-line arguments via the sys.argv list, where sys.argv[0] is the script name, and subsequent elements are the arguments passed by the user. Here's an example of a script that takes a filename as a command-line argument:

```python
import sys


if len(sys.argv) != 2:

    print("Usage: python script.py <filename>")

    sys.exit(1)


filename = sys.argv[1]

print(f"Processing file: {filename}")
```

In this example, the script checks that exactly one argument (besides the script name) is provided. If not, it displays a usage message and exits. If the correct number of arguments is provided, the script proceeds to process the filename.

The argparse module offers a powerful and flexible way to define and parse arguments for more sophisticated command-line interfaces. The argparse module allows you to specify argument names, types, default values, and help messages, making it easier to handle complex input requirements. Here's an example of using argparse to create a script with multiple options:

```python
import argparse

parser = argparse.ArgumentParser(description="A simple file processing script.")

parser.add_argument("filename", type=str, help="The name of the file to process.")

parser.add_argument("--verbose", action="store_true", help="Enable verbose output.")

parser.add_argument("--count", type=int, default=1, help="Number of times to process the file.")


args = parser.parse_args()


print(f"Processing file: {args.filename}")

if args.verbose:

  print("Verbose mode enabled.")

print(f"Processing {args.count} times.")
```

In this example, argparse is used to define a required positional argument (filename), an optional boolean flag (--verbose), and an optional integer argument with a default value (--count). The parse_args() method parses the command-line arguments and stores them in the args object, which can then be accessed within the script.

In addition to command-line interfaces, graphical user interfaces (GUIs) provide a more user-friendly way to capture input from users. Python offers several libraries for creating GUIs, including Tkinter, PyQt, and Kivy. Tkinter is the standard GUI toolkit for Python and is included with most Python installations. It provides a straightforward way to create windows, dialogs, and input widgets. Here's an example of a simple Tkinter application that captures user input:

```python
import tkinter as tk

from tkinter import messagebox


def submit():

    name = entry.get()

    messagebox.showinfo("Input Received", f"Hello, {name}!")


root = tk.Tk()

root.title("User Input Example")


label = tk.Label(root, text="Enter your name:")

label.pack(pady=10)


entry = tk.Entry(root)

entry.pack(pady=5)
```

```python
button = tk.Button(root, text="Submit", command=submit)

button.pack(pady=20)


root.mainloop()
```

In this example, a Tkinter window is created with a label, an entry widget for user input, and a button to submit the input. When the button is clicked, the submit() function retrieves the input from the entry widget and displays it in a message box. This approach provides a simple and intuitive way for users to interact with the application.

Python's flexibility in handling user input extends to web applications as well. Frameworks such as Flask and Django allow developers to create web applications that capture user input through HTML forms. Flask, a lightweight web framework, provides an easy way to define routes and handle form submissions. Here's an example of a simple Flask application that captures user input from a web form:

```python
from flask import Flask, request, render_template_string


app = Flask(__name__)


@app.route("/", methods=["GET", "POST"])

def index():

  if request.method == "POST":

    name = request.form["name"]

    return f"Hello, {name}!"

  return render_template_string("""
```

```python
        <form method="post">

            Enter your name: <input type="text" name="name">
            <input type="submit">

        </form>

    ''')

if __name__ == "__main__":

  app.run(debug=True)
```

In this example, the Flask application defines a route for the root URL ("/") and handles both GET and POST requests. The HTML form is rendered using a template string, and when the form is submitted, the input is captured from the request.form dictionary and displayed to the user.

Getting user input is fundamental to interactive programming, enabling dynamic and responsive applications. Whether through basic console input, command-line arguments, graphical user interfaces, or web forms, Python provides a rich set of tools and techniques for capturing and validating user input. By understanding and effectively using these methods, developers can create robust and user-friendly applications that meet the needs of their users. Whether for simple scripts or complex systems, the ability to handle user input is a vital skill in Python programming, ensuring that applications are flexible, interactive, and capable of responding to user actions.

CHAPTER III

Making Decisions and Looping

Introduction to Conditional Statements

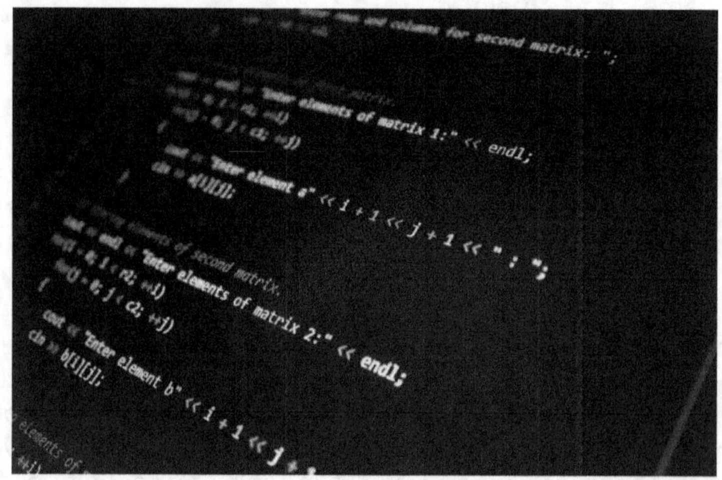

Conditional statements are a fundamental concept in programming, allowing your program to make decisions based on certain conditions. Imagine if your favorite video game character always did the same thing no matter what obstacles they faced. It wouldn't be fascinating, would it? Conditional statements let your character decide when to jump, duck, and run based on what's happening in the game. This is what makes programs dynamic and interactive, just like your favorite games.

In Python, conditional statements are created using the if, elif, and else keywords. These keywords help your program to choose between different actions based on certain conditions. Let's start with the simplest conditional statement, the if statement. Think of the if statement as a question that your program asks. If the answer is "yes," the program does something special. For example, if you wanted to write a program that checks if you have enough money to buy an ice cream, you would use an if statement to make that decision.

Here's a simple example:

money = 10

if money >= 5:

    print("You can buy an ice cream!")

In this program, the variable money is set to 10. The if statement checks if money is greater than or equal to 5. Since 10 is greater than 5, the program prints "You can buy an ice cream!" If money was less than 5, the program wouldn't print anything because the condition wouldn't be met.

But what if you want your program to do something different when the condition is not met? That's where the else statement comes in. The else statement provides an alternative action when the if condition is false. Continuing with our ice cream example, we can add an else statement to handle the situation when you don't have enough money:

money = 3

if money >= 5:

    print("You can buy an ice cream!")

else:

    print("You don't have enough money for an ice cream.")

Now, if money is set to 3, the program will print "You don't have enough money for an ice cream." This is because 3 is not greater than or equal to 5, so the else statement provides an alternative message. Sometimes, you might have more than two possibilities to check. This is where the elif statement comes in handy. Elif stands for "else if" and allows you to check multiple conditions sequentially. For instance, let's say you want to write a program that checks your grades and prints a message based on the grade:

```python
grade = 85

if grade >= 90:

    print("You got an A!")

elif grade >= 80:

    print("You got a B!")

elif grade >= 70:

    print("You got a C!")

elif grade >= 60:

    print("You got a D!")

else:

    print("You got an F.")
```

In this example, the program checks your grade and prints a different message depending on the range in which your grade falls. If grade is 85, the program prints "You got a B!" because 85 is greater than or equal to 80 but less than 90. The elif statements provide additional conditions to check, and the else statement catches any remaining possibilities.

Let's consider a more interactive example. Suppose you're creating a simple game where the player can choose different actions based on their energy level.

Here's how you might use conditional statements to determine what the player can do:

```python
energy = 50

if energy > 80:

    print("You are full of energy! You can run, jump, and explore!")

elif energy > 50:

    print("You have enough energy to walk and explore.")

elif energy > 20:

    print("You are getting tired. You should rest soon.")

else:

    print("You are exhausted! You need to rest.")
```

In this game, the player's energy level determines their actions. If their energy is above 80, they can do various activities. They can walk and explore if their energy is between 51 and 80. If their energy is between 21 and 50, they are getting tired and should rest soon. If their energy is 20 or below, they need to rest immediately.

Now, let's add a twist to our game. Suppose we want to give the player the option to find food and regain energy. We can use nested conditional statements to handle this situation. Nested conditional statements are if, elif, and else statements inside another if, elif, or else block. Here's how we might add this feature:

```python
energy = 30
found_food = True

if energy > 80:
```

```python
    print("You are full of energy! You can run, jump, and explore!")

elif energy > 50:

    print("You have enough energy to walk and explore.")

elif energy > 20:

    if found_food:

        print("You are getting tired. But you found some food and regained energy!")

        energy += 30

    else:

        print("You are getting tired. You should rest soon.")

else:

    print("You are exhausted! You need to rest.")
```

In this example, if the player's energy is between 21 and 50 and they find food (found_food is True), the program prints a message saying they regained energy and increases their energy by 30. This adds more depth to the game and shows how nested conditional statements can make your programs more interactive and dynamic. Understanding conditional statements is key to writing interactive programs that respond to different situations. They are like the decision-making parts of your program, allowing it to react differently based on the input it receives. Whether you're creating a game, building a calculator, or writing a chatbot, conditional statements are an essential tool in your programming toolbox. Let's look at another fun example that combines conditional statements with user input. Suppose you're building a simple chatbot that greets users based on the time of day. You can use input() to get the user's name and the current hour, and then use conditional statements to print an appropriate greeting:

```python
name = input("What's your name? ")

hour = int(input("What hour is it (0-23)? "))


if 5 <= hour < 12:

    print(f"Good morning, {name}!")

elif 12 <= hour < 18:

    print(f"Good afternoon, {name}!")

elif 18 <= hour < 22:

    print(f"Good evening, {name}!")

else:

    print(f"Good night, {name}!")
```

The program asks for the user's name and current hour in this chatbot. It then uses conditional statements to print a different greeting depending on the time of day. It prints a morning greeting if the hour is between 5 and 11. It prints an afternoon greeting if the hour is between 12 and 17. It prints an evening greeting if the hour is between 18 and 21. For any other time, it prints a night greeting. This makes the chatbot feel more personalized and responsive. Conditional statements are also important for making decisions based on multiple conditions using logical operators. Logical operators such as and, or, and not allow you to combine multiple conditions in a single if statement. For example, let's say you're writing a program to check if a user is eligible for a discount. The user is eligible if they are a student or a senior citizen and if they have a membership card:

```python
is_student = True

is_senior = False

has_membership_card = True


if (is_student or is_senior) and has_membership_card:

    print("You are eligible for a discount!")

else:

    print("You are not eligible for a discount.")
```

In this example, the user is eligible for a discount if they are either a student or a senior citizen and they have a membership card. The or operator checks if either is_student or is_senior is True, and the and operator checks if has_membership_card is True. If both conditions are met, the program prints a message saying the user is eligible for a discount.

Learning to use conditional statements is fundamental to becoming a proficient programmer. They allow you to control the flow of your program and make it interactive and responsive to different inputs and conditions. Mastering conditional statements allows you to create more complex and engaging programs that can handle various scenarios.

In conclusion, conditional statements are like the decision-making brains of your programs. They help your code decide what to do based on the conditions you set. With if, elif, and else statements, you can guide your programs to make the right choices and respond appropriately to user input and other conditions. Mastering conditional statements will enable you to write dynamic and flexible code, whether you are building a game, a chatbot, or any interactive application. As you practice and experiment with these concepts, you'll find that your programs become more powerful and engaging, just like the games and applications you love to use.

Using Loops

Imagine playing a game where you must collect 100 coins to win. It would be really boring to have to write down "I collected a coin" 100 times. This is where loops come in handy. Loops are a fundamental concept in programming that allows you to repeat a block of code multiple times without writing it repeatedly. There are two main types of loops in Python: for loops and while loops. Understanding how to use these loops can make your programs more efficient and easier to write.

Let's start with for loops. A for loop is used when you want to repeat a block of code a certain number of times or iterate over a sequence, such as a list or a string. Think of a for loop as a way to say, "Do this action for every item in this list" or "Do this action this many times." For example, if you want to print the numbers from 1 to 5, you can use a for loop:

```
for i in range(1, 6):

    print(i)
```

In this example, the range(1, 6) function generates a sequence of numbers from 1 to 5. The for loop iterates over this sequence, assigning each number to the variable i and printing it. This means the print(i) line runs five times, once for each number in the sequence. Using a for loop saves you from having to write print(1), print(2), print(3), and so on.

For loops are also great for working with lists. Suppose you have a list of your favorite fruits, and you want to print each one:

```
fruits = ["apple", "banana", "cherry"]
```

```
for fruit in fruits:

    print(fruit)
```

In this case, the for loop goes through each fruit list item. The variable fruit takes on the value of each item, one at a time, and the print(fruit) line runs for each item. So the program prints "apple", "banana", and "cherry" in sequence.

Now let's talk about while loops. A while loop is used when you want to repeat a block of code as long as a certain condition is true. It's like saying, "Keep doing this action while this condition is true." For example, if you want to print numbers from 1 to 5 using a while loop, you can do it like this:

```
i = 1

while i <= 5:

    print(i)

    i += 1
```

In this example, the loop starts with i set to 1. The while loop checks if i is less than or equal to 5. If it is, the loop runs, printing i and then increasing i by 1 using the i += 1 statement. This process repeats until i becomes 6, at which point the condition i <= 5 is no longer true, and the loop stops.

While loops are particularly useful when you don't know in advance how many times you need to repeat the block of code. For instance, you might want to keep asking users for input until they enter a specific word. Here's an example where the program keeps asking for a password until the correct one is entered:

```
password = ""

while password != "letmein":
```

```python
password = input("Enter the password: ")

print("Access granted!")
```

In this example, the while loop checks if the entered password is not equal to "letmein". If it's not, the loop runs, asking the user to enter the password again. This continues until the user types "letmein", when the loop stops, and the program prints "Access granted!".

Sometimes, you might want to stop a loop early or skip over certain parts of the loop. Python provides two special keywords for this: break and continue. The break keyword is used to exit the loop immediately, even if the loop condition is still true. For example, if you are searching for a particular number in a list and want to stop as soon as you find it, you can use break:

```python
numbers = [1, 2, 3, 4, 5]
for number in numbers:
    if number == 3:
        print("Found 3!")
        break
    print(number)
```

In this example, the for loop iterates over the numbers list. When it finds the number 3, it prints "Found 3!" and then exits the loop using break. The print(number) statement only runs for the numbers before 3.

The continue keyword is used to skip the rest of the code inside the loop for the current iteration and move to the next iteration. For example, if you want to print all the numbers from 1 to 5 except for 3, you can use continue:

```python
for i in range(1, 6):
    if i == 3:
```

```
    continue

  print(i)
```

In this example, the for loop goes through numbers 1 to 5. When it reaches 3, it skips the print(i) statement and moves to the following number. So, the program prints 1, 2, 4, and 5, but not 3.

Loops can also be nested, meaning you can have a loop inside another loop. This is useful for working with multi-dimensional data, like a grid or a table. For example, if you want to print a multiplication table, you can use nested loops:

```
for i in range(1, 6):

  for j in range(1, 6):

    print(i * j, end="\t")

  print()
```

In this example, the outer for loop iterates over the numbers from 1 to 5, and the inner for loop does the same. The print(i * j, end="\t") statement prints the product of i and j, followed by a tab character to separate the numbers. After the inner loop, the print() statement ensures that each row of the multiplication table is printed on a new line.

Loops are potent tools in programming because they allow you to automate repetitive tasks, process data, and build complex algorithms. They are used in everything from simple calculations to advanced simulations. For example, in a game, loops can be used to keep the game running, update the position of characters, check for collisions, and so on.

Let's consider a practical example where loops can be used to solve a problem. Suppose you want to write a program that calculates the factorial of a number. The factorial of a number is the product of all positive integers less than or equal to that number. For example, the factorial of 5 (written as 5!) is 5 * 4 * 3 * 2 * 1, which equals 120. You can use a for loop to calculate the factorial:

```python
number = int(input("Enter a number: "))

factorial = 1


for i in range(1, number + 1):

    factorial *= i


print(f"The factorial of {number} is {factorial}")
```

In this example, the for loop iterates over the numbers from 1 to number. The variable factorial starts at 1 and is multiplied by each number in the loop. After the loop finishes, the program prints the result. This is a simple yet powerful use of loops to perform a mathematical calculation.

Another example where loops are useful is in data processing. Suppose you have a list of test scores and you want to calculate the average score. You can use a for loop to sum the scores and then divide by the number of scores:

```python
scores = [85, 90, 78, 92, 88]

total = 0


for score in scores:

    total += score
```

average = total / len(scores)

print(f"The average score is {average}")

In this example, the for loop iterates over the scores list, adding each score to the total. After the loop finishes, the average is calculated by dividing the total by the number of scores. This demonstrates how loops can be used to process data and perform calculations.

Loops are not only useful for numbers and lists; they can also be used with strings. For example, you might want to count the number of vowels in a word. You can use a for loop to iterate over the characters in the word and check if each character is a vowel:

word = "programming"

vowel_count = 0

vowels = "aeiou"

for char in word:

  if char in vowels:

    vowel_count += 1

print(f"The number of vowels in '{word}' is {vowel_count}")

In this example, the for loop iterates over each character in the word "programming". The if statement checks if the character is in the string "aeiou". If it is, the vowel_count is incremented. This shows how loops can be used to analyze and manipulate strings.

In conclusion, loops are an essential part of programming that allows you to repeat actions, process data, and build complex algorithms efficiently. Whether you are using for loops to iterate over sequences or while loops to repeat actions based on conditions, understanding how to use loops effectively can make your programs more powerful and easier to write. By practicing and experimenting with loops, you will discover many ways to simplify tasks, automate repetitive actions, and create more dynamic and interactive programs. As you continue to learn and explore, loops will become one of the most valuable tools in your programming toolkit, enabling you to easily solve problems and create exciting projects.

Loop Control Statements (break, continue)

Imagine you're on a treasure hunt, and you have a map that tells you to look for clues at various spots. Sometimes, you might find a clue that tells you to stop searching because you've found the treasure. Other times, you might find something that tells you to skip the current spot and move on to the next one. In programming, we have something similar called loop control statements. These special commands help us control the flow of loops, allowing us to stop the loop early or skip parts of it based on certain conditions. The two most commonly used loop control statements in Python are break and continue.

Let's start with the break statement. The break statement is like finding the treasure and stopping the hunt immediately. When Python encounters a break statement inside a loop, it stops the loop entirely, no matter its condition. This can be very useful when you want to exit a loop early because you've found what you're looking for, or there's no need to continue.

For example, suppose you're searching for a specific number in a list, and you want to stop the search as soon as you find it. Here's how you might use the break statement:

```python
numbers = [1, 3, 5, 7, 9, 11]

target = 7


for number in numbers:

    if number == target:

        print("Found the number!")

        break

    print(f"Checked number {number}")


print("Search complete.")
```

In this example, the loop goes through each number in the list. When it finds the target number (7), it prints "Found the number!" the break statement immediately stops the loop. The message "Checked number" is printed for each number that is checked until the target is found. After the loop, the program prints "Search complete." Without the break statement, the loop would continue checking all the numbers in the list, even after finding the target.

Now let's look at the continue statement. The continue statement is like finding a clue that tells you to skip the current spot and move on to the next one. When Python encounters a continue statement inside a loop, it skips the rest of the code inside the loop for the current iteration and goes straight to the next iteration.

For example, suppose you want to print all the numbers from 1 to 10, but you want to skip the number 5. Here's how you might use the continue statement:

```python
for i in range(1, 11):
```

```python
if i == 5:

    continue

print(i)
```

In this example, the loop goes through numbers 1 to 10. When it reaches the number 5, the continue statement tells Python to skip the print(i) statement for that iteration and move on to the following number. So, the program prints all the numbers from 1 to 10 except 5.

Using break and continue can make your programs more efficient and easier to read by avoiding unnecessary computations and focusing on the essential parts of the loop. They are beneficial in situations where you need to handle special cases or optimize performance.

Let's consider another example where both break and continue can be useful. Suppose you are playing a game where you need to find hidden keys in different rooms, but some rooms are locked, and you want to skip them. Also, if you find a key, you want to stop searching immediately. Here's how you might use break and continue in this scenario:

```python
rooms = ["empty", "locked", "empty", "key", "empty", "locked", "empty"]

for room in rooms:
    if room == "locked":
        print("Skipping a locked room.")
        continue
    if room == "key":
        print("Found the key!")
```

```python
        break

    print("Searching an empty room.")

print("Search ended.")
```

In this example, the loop goes through each room in the list. If it finds a locked room, the continue statement skips the rest of the loop for that iteration and moves on to the next room. If it finds a room with a key, the break statement stops the loop immediately. The program prints messages indicating whether it's skipping a locked room, searching an empty room, or finding the key. After the loop, the program prints "Search ended."

Sometimes, you might use nested loops, which are loops inside other loops. In such cases, break and continue can help you control the flow of the inner loops without affecting the outer loop. For example, suppose you are creating a multiplication table, but you want to skip multiplying by a certain number and stop the table early if a product exceeds a certain value. Here's how you might use break and continue with nested loops:

```python
skip_number = 3
stop_value = 50

for i in range(1, 6):
    for j in range(1, 6):
        if j == skip_number:
            continue
        product = i * j
        if product > stop_value:
```

```python
        break

    print(f"{i} * {j} = {product}")
```

In this example, the outer loop goes through the numbers 1 to 5, and the inner loop does the same. If the inner loop encounters the skip number (3), the continue statement skips the multiplication for that iteration. If the product of i and j exceeds the stop value (50), the break statement stops the inner loop immediately. The program prints the multiplication results, skipping certain products and stopping early when necessary.

Another practical use of break and continue is in handling user input. Suppose you are writing a program that asks the user to enter positive numbers, and the program stops asking when the user enters a negative number. Here's how you might use break in this scenario:

```python
while True:

    number = int(input("Enter a positive number (or a negative number to stop): "))

    if number < 0:

        break

    print(f"You entered: {number}")

print("Program ended.")
```

In this example, the while loop runs indefinitely, asking the user to enter a positive number. The break statement stops the loop if the user enters a negative number. The program prints the entered number for each positive input and ends with the message "Program ended." Similarly, you might want to skip over certain inputs, such as ignoring zero values while calculating the sum of numbers. Here's how you might use continue in this scenario:

```python
total = 0

while True:
    number = int(input("Enter a number (or a negative number to stop): "))
    if number < 0:
        break
    if number == 0:
        continue
    total += number

print(f"The total sum is: {total}")
```

In this example, the while loop continues to ask the user for input until a negative number is entered. If the user enters zero, the continue statement skips adding zero to the total sum and moves on to the next iteration. The program calculates and prints the total sum of all non-zero positive numbers the user enters.

Understanding and using break and continue effectively can make your programs more flexible and efficient. They allow you to handle special cases, optimize performance, and control the flow of loops clearly and concisely. By practicing with these loop control statements, you will develop the skills to write more powerful and dynamic programs.

In conclusion, break and continue are essential tools in a programmer's toolkit for controlling the flow of loops. The break statement allows you to exit a loop early when a specific condition is met, while the continue statement lets you skip the rest of the current iteration and move on to the next one. These statements can be used in various scenarios, from searching lists and handling user input to managing nested loops and optimizing performance. By mastering break and continue, you can create more efficient, readable, and dynamic programs that respond appropriately to different situations. As you continue to explore and practice these concepts, you will find that they greatly enhance your ability to solve problems and write effective code.

CHAPTER IV

Functions and Data Structures

Introduction to Functions

Imagine you are building a LEGO castle. Each part of the castle, like the towers, walls, and gates, can be built separately and then assembled together to form the whole structure. Functions in programming are like those individual LEGO pieces. They allow you to break down a big task into smaller, manageable parts that you can work on separately and then combine to complete the whole task. In Python, functions help you organize your code, make it reusable, and keep it clean and easy to understand.

A function is a block of code that performs a specific task. You can think of it as a mini-program within your main program. Functions allow you to write a piece of code once and then use it whenever you need it, without having to rewrite the same code repeatedly. This is not only time-saving but also reduces the chances of making errors. For example, if you are writing a game and need to calculate the player's score multiple times, you can write a function for this calculation and call it whenever required.

Creating a function in Python involves two main steps: defining the function and calling the function. To define a function, you use the def keyword followed by the function name and parentheses. Inside the parentheses, you can specify parameters like placeholders for the values the function will work with. After the function name and parameters, you write a colon (:) and then the

indented block of code that makes up the function body. Here's an example of a simple function that prints a greeting:
def greet():

    print("Hello, welcome to the world of Python!")

In this example, def is used to define the function named greet. The function doesn't take any parameters and simply prints a message when called. To use this function, you call it by writing its name followed by parentheses, like this:

greet()

When this line of code runs, the function prints "Hello, welcome to the world of Python!" to the screen.

Functions can also take parameters, allowing them to perform tasks with different inputs. Parameters are specified inside the parentheses when defining the function. For example, let's modify the greet function to take a name as a parameter and print a personalized greeting:

def greet(name):

    print(f"Hello, {name}, welcome to the world of Python!")

Now, when you call the function, you need to provide a value for the name parameter:

greet("Alice")

greet("Bob")

In these calls, the function prints "Hello, Alice, welcome to the world of Python!" and "Hello, Bob, welcome to the world of Python!" respectively. Using parameters makes your functions more flexible and powerful, as they can work with different values each time they are called.

Functions can also return values. A return value is the result that a function gives back after completing its task. To return a value from a function, you use the return keyword followed by the value you want to return. Here's an example of a function that adds two numbers and returns the result:

```python
def add(a, b):

    return a + b
```

In this example, the function add takes two parameters, a and b, adds them together, and returns the sum. To use this function and get the result, you can call it and store the returned value in a variable:

```python
result = add(3, 5)

print(result)
```

This code prints 8 because the add function returns the sum of 3 and 5. Returning values from functions is very useful when you need to perform calculations or process data and then use the result in other parts of your program.

Sometimes, you might need a function to do multiple things before returning a value. For example, let's write a function that calculates the area of a rectangle. The function takes the length and width of the rectangle as parameters, calculates the area, and then returns it:

```python
def calculate_area(length, width):

    area = length * width

    return area
```

To use this function, you call it with the length and width of the rectangle and store the result:

```python
rectangle_area = calculate_area(10, 5)
```

```python
print(f"The area of the rectangle is: {rectangle_area}")
```

This code prints "The area of the rectangle is: 50" because the function calculates the area as 10 * 5 and returns 50.

Functions can also call other functions, which allows you to build more complex behavior by combining simpler functions. For example, let's write a function that calculates the perimeter of a rectangle and then use it along with the calculate_area function to print both the area and the perimeter:

```python
def calculate_perimeter(length, width):

    perimeter = 2 * (length + width)

    return perimeter


def display_rectangle_info(length, width):

    area = calculate_area(length, width)

    perimeter = calculate_perimeter(length, width)

    print(f"The area of the rectangle is: {area}")

    print(f"The perimeter of the rectangle is: {perimeter}")


display_rectangle_info(10, 5)
```

In this example, display_rectangle_info calls both calculate_area and calculate_perimeter, gets their results, and prints them. Breaking down the task into smaller functions makes the code more organized and easier to understand.

Another useful feature of functions is that they can have default parameters. Default parameters allow you to specify a default value for a parameter, which is used if no value is provided when the function is called. This makes your functions more flexible and easier to use. Here's an example of a function with a default parameter:

```python
def greet(name="stranger"):

  print(f"Hello, {name}, welcome to the world of Python!")
```

Now, you can call greet with or without a parameter:

```python
greet("Alice")

greet()
```

The first call prints "Hello, Alice, welcome to the world of Python!" and the second call prints "Hello, stranger, welcome to the world of Python!" because the default value "stranger" is used when no parameter is provided.

Functions can also take a variable number of arguments using the *args syntax. This is useful when you don't know in advance how many arguments a function will need to handle. For example, let's write a function that calculates the sum of an arbitrary number of numbers:

```python
def sum_all(*args):
  total = 0
  for number in args:
    total += number
  return total
```

In this function, *args collects all the arguments passed to the function into a tuple. The loop goes through each number in args and adds it to the total. You can call sum_all with any number of arguments:

```python
print(sum_all(1, 2, 3))

print(sum_all(5, 10, 15, 20))
```

The first call prints 6 because the sum of 1, 2, and 3 is 6. The second call prints 50 because the sum of 5, 10, 15, and 20 is 50. Using *args makes your functions more flexible and adaptable to different situations.

Understanding and using functions is a key skill in programming. They help you organize your code, make it reusable, and keep it clean and easy to understand. Functions allow you to break down complex tasks into smaller, manageable parts, making your programs easier to write, debug, and maintain. By practicing with functions, you will develop the ability to write more efficient, modular, and powerful code.

Let's look at one more example to see how functions can be used to create a simple game. Suppose you want to write a guessing game where the player has to guess a number between 1 and 100. You can use functions to handle different parts of the game, such as getting the player's guess, checking if the guess is correct, and giving feedback. Here's a simple version of the game:

```python
import random


def get_guess():

    return int(input("Enter your guess: "))


def check_guess(guess, target):

    if guess < target:
        print("Too low!")
    elif guess > target:
        print("Too high!")
    else:
```

```python
    print("Congratulations! You guessed it!")

def play_game():

  target = random.randint(1, 100)

  guess = None


  while guess != target:

    guess = get_guess()

    check_guess(guess, target)


play_game()
```

In this game, the get_guess function gets the player's guess, the check_guess function checks if the guess is correct and gives feedback, and the play_game function manages the game loop. By using functions, the code is organized into clear, logical parts, making it easier to understand and modify.

In conclusion, functions are a powerful Python tool that allows you to organize your code, make it reusable, and keep it clean and easy to understand. They help you break down complex tasks into smaller, manageable parts and perform specific actions with different inputs. By mastering functions, you can create more efficient, modular, and powerful programs, making your coding experience more enjoyable and productive. So, start practicing with functions today and discover how they can transform your programming projects!

Using Lists and Tuples

Imagine you are organizing a birthday party and you need to keep track of all the things you need to buy and the games you want to play. You might write everything down on a piece of paper in a list format. In programming, we have something similar called lists and tuples. They help us store collections of items in an organized way so we can access and use them easily. In Python, lists and tuples are very useful tools that help us manage and manipulate groups of related data.

A list in Python is like a collection of items that you can change, add to, or remove from as you need. Think of it as a shopping list you can update whenever possible. To create a list, you use square brackets and separate the items with commas. Here is an example of a simple list:

```
shopping_list = ["apples", "bananas", "milk", "bread"]
```

This list has four items: apples, bananas, milk, and bread. Each item is a string, and they are all stored in a specific order. You can access each item in the list by using its index, which is the position of the item in the list. The index starts at 0, so the first item is at index 0, the second item is at index 1, and so on. For example, if you want to print the first item in the shopping list, you can do this:

```
print(shopping_list[0])
```

This code will print "apples" because "apples" is the first item in the list. If you want to print the second item, you use index 1:

```
print(shopping_list[1])
```

This will print "bananas". You can also use negative indexes to access items from the end of the list. For example, -1 refers to the last item, -2 refers to the second-to-last item, and so on:

```
print(shopping_list[-1])
```

This will print "bread".

One of the best things about lists is that they are mutable, which means you can change them after they are created. You can add new items, remove items, or modify existing items. For example, to add an item to the end of the list, you can use the append method:

```
shopping_list.append("eggs")

print(shopping_list)
```

This will add "eggs" to the end of the list and print ["apples", "bananas", "milk", "bread", "eggs"]. If you want to insert an item at a specific position, you can use the insert method:

```
shopping_list.insert(2, "cheese")

print(shopping_list)
```

This will insert "cheese" at index 2 and print ["apples", "bananas", "cheese", "milk", "bread", "eggs"]. To remove an item, you can use the remove method:

```
shopping_list.remove("milk")

print(shopping_list)
```

This will remove "milk" from the list and print ["apples", "bananas", "cheese", "bread", "eggs"].

Another useful feature of lists is that you can loop through them to perform actions on each item. For example, if you want to print each item in the shopping list, you can use a for loop:

```
for item in shopping_list:
    print(item)
```

This will print each item on a new line. Lists are also great for storing related data you want to process together. For example, if you have a list of numbers, you can use loops and built-in functions to perform calculations on the list. Here's an example where we calculate the total and average of a list of numbers:

```
numbers = [5, 10, 15, 20, 25]
total = sum(numbers)
average = total / len(numbers)
print(f"Total: {total}, Average: {average}")
```

This code calculates the sum of the numbers using the sum function, calculates the average by dividing the total by the number of items in the list using the len function, and prints the results.

Now, let's talk about tuples. A tuple is similar to a list in that it can store multiple items, but there is one key difference: tuples are immutable. This means that once you create a tuple, you cannot change it, add to it, or remove items from it. Think of a tuple like a list of friends attending your birthday party. Once you send out the invitations, the list of invited friends is fixed. To create a tuple, you use parentheses instead of square brackets:

```
birthday_guests = ("Alice", "Bob", "Charlie")
```

We have three guests in this tuple: Alice, Bob, and Charlie. You can access the items in a tuple like you access items in a list, using their indexes. For example, to print the first guest, you do this:

```
print(birthday_guests[0])
```

This will print "Alice". You can also use negative indexes to access items from the end of the tuple:

```
print(birthday_guests[-1])
```

This will print "Charlie".

Even though you cannot change the items in a tuple, tuples are still very useful in many situations. They are often used to store collections of items that should not change throughout the program, such as coordinates, days of the week, or months of the year. For example, if you are writing a program that needs to use the days of the week, you can store them in a tuple:

days_of_week = ("Sunday", "Monday", "Tuesday", "Wednesday", "Thursday", "Friday", "Saturday")

You can then access the days using their indexes just like you would with a list. Tuples are also useful for returning multiple values from a function. For example, let's say you have a function that calculates a rectangle's area and perimeter. You can return both values as a tuple:

```python
def rectangle_info(length, width):
    area = length * width
    perimeter = 2 * (length + width)
    return (area, perimeter)

info = rectangle_info(10, 5)
print(f"Area: {info[0]}, Perimeter: {info[1]}")
```

In this example, the rectangle_info function calculates the area and perimeter of a rectangle and returns them as a tuple. You can then access the returned values using their indexes.

Both lists and tuples are potent tools that can help you manage data collections in your programs. They each have their strengths and are suited to different types of tasks. Lists are great when you need a collection of items that you can change, add to, or remove from. Tuples are perfect for collections of items that should not change and for situations where you want to return multiple values from a function.

One important concept when working with lists and tuples is the idea of slicing. Slicing allows you to access a part of the list or tuple by specifying a range of indexes. For example, if you have a list of numbers and you want to get the first three numbers, you can use slicing:

numbers = [10, 20, 30, 40, 50]
first_three = numbers[:3]
print(first_three)

This will print [10, 20, 30]. The [:3] syntax means "start from the beginning and go up to, but not including, index 3". You can also specify a starting index and an ending index:

middle_numbers = numbers[1:4]
print(middle_numbers)

This will print [20, 30, 40]. The [1:4] syntax means "start from index 1 and go up to, but not including, index 4". Slicing works with both lists and tuples and is very useful for extracting specific parts of your data.

Another useful feature of lists is that they can contain other lists. This is called a nested list. Nested lists are useful for representing more complex data structures like grids or tables. For example, if you are writing a program to represent a tic-tac-toe board, you can use a nested list:

tic_tac_toe_board = [

    ["X", "O", "X"],
    ["O", "X", "O"],
    ["X", "X", "O"]

```python
]

for row in tic_tac_toe_board:

    for cell in row:

        print(cell, end=" ")

    print()
```

This code creates a nested list representing the tic-tac-toe board and uses nested for loops to print each cell. The end=" " parameter in the print function keeps the cells in the same row on the same line, and the second print function adds a new line after each row.

In conclusion, lists and tuples are essential tools in Python that help you store and manage data collections. Lists are mutable and allow you to change, add, or remove items, making them perfect for tasks that require flexibility. Tuples are immutable and are great for storing collections of items that should not change. Both lists and tuples can be accessed using indexes and sliced to get specific parts of the data. You can write more efficient, organized, and powerful programs by understanding how to use lists and tuples. So, start practicing with lists and tuples today and discover how they can help you manage your data and build amazing projects!

Working with Dictionaries and Sets

Imagine you are organizing a big treasure hunt with your friends. You have a map with different locations marked; each location has a clue leading to the next place. You need a way to store the locations and their corresponding clues so that you can easily look them up when needed. In programming, we have a tool called a dictionary that helps us similarly store data. Another helpful tool is a set, which allows us keep track of unique items, like a list of all the different treasures found during the hunt. Let's dive into how dictionaries and sets work in Python and how they can help us manage and organize data efficiently.

A dictionary in Python is like a real-life dictionary where you look up words to find their meanings. In Python, a dictionary stores data as key-value pairs. The key is like the word you are looking up, and the value is like the definition. To create a dictionary, you use curly braces {} and separate keys and values with a colon :. Here's an example of a simple dictionary that stores the ages of some friends:

```python
ages = {

    "Alice": 12,

    "Bob": 14,

    "Charlie": 13

}
```

In this dictionary, "Alice", "Bob", and "Charlie" are the keys, and their ages (12, 14, and 13) are the values. You can access the value associated with a key by using square brackets []. For example, to get Alice's age, you do this:

```python
print(ages["Alice"])
```

This code will print 12 because that is the value associated with the key "Alice". If you want to add a new friend to the dictionary, you can simply assign a value to a new key:

```python
ages["David"] = 15

print(ages)
```

This will add "David" with the age 15 to the dictionary, and the updated dictionary will be {"Alice": 12, "Bob": 14, "Charlie": 13, "David": 15}. If you want to update the age of an existing friend, you just assign a new value to the key:

```
ages["Alice"] = 13
```

```
print(ages)
```

This will change Alice's age to 13, and the updated dictionary will be {"Alice": 13, "Bob": 14, "Charlie": 13, "David": 15}.

Dictionaries are powerful because they allow you to quickly store and retrieve data using keys. You can also check if a key exists in a dictionary using the in keyword:

```
if "Eve" in ages:

    print("Eve's age is", ages["Eve"])

else:

    print("Eve is not in the dictionary")
```

This code checks if "Eve" is a key in the dictionary and prints a message accordingly. Since "Eve" is not in the dictionary, it will print "Eve is not in the dictionary".

Dictionaries are also great for organizing more complex data. For example, suppose you are organizing a school fair and must keep track of the different booths and their activities. You can use a dictionary to store this information:

```
fair_booths = {

  "Games": ["Ring Toss", "Balloon Darts", "Duck Pond"],

  "Food": ["Hot Dogs", "Cotton Candy", "Popcorn"],
```

   "Crafts": ["Face Painting", "Bracelet Making", "Origami"]

}

In this dictionary, each key is a booth category, and the value is a list of activities at that booth. You can access the list of activities for a booth by using its key:

print(fair_booths["Games"])

This code will print ["Ring Toss", "Balloon Darts", "Duck Pond"]. If you want to add a new activity to a booth, you can use the append method on the list:

fair_booths["Games"].append("Sack Race")

print(fair_booths["Games"])

This will add "Sack Race" to the list of games and print ["Ring Toss", "Balloon Darts", "Duck Pond", "Sack Race"].

Now let's talk about sets. A set in Python is like a collection of unique items, just like a bag of different treasures where no two items are the same. To create a set, you use curly braces {} just like with dictionaries, but without key-value pairs. Here's an example of a simple set that stores some unique numbers:

unique_numbers = {1, 2, 3, 4, 5}

In this set, we have five numbers, each unique. If you try to add a duplicate item to the set, it will not be added because sets do not allow duplicates. For example, if you try to add the number 3 to the set again, it will have no effect:

unique_numbers.add(3)
print(unique_numbers)

This code will still print {1, 2, 3, 4, 5} because 3 is already in the set.

Sets are very useful for keeping track of unique items and performing operations like finding the union, intersection, and difference of sets. For example, suppose you have two sets of treasures found by two different teams during the treasure hunt:

team_a_treasures = {"gold coin", "silver coin", "pearl"}

team_b_treasures = {"silver coin", "emerald", "ruby"}

You can find the union of the two sets, which is all the unique treasures found by both teams, using the union method or the | operator:

all_treasures = team_a_treasures.union(team_b_treasures)
print(all_treasures)

This will print {"gold coin", "silver coin", "pearl", "emerald", "ruby"}. You can also find the intersection of the two sets, which is the treasures found by both teams, using the intersection method or the & operator:

common_treasures = team_a_treasures.intersection(team_b_treasures)

print(common_treasures)

This will print {"silver coin"} because "silver coin" is the only treasure found by both teams. If you want to find the treasures found by team A but not by team B, you can use the difference method or the - operator:

unique_to_team_a = team_a_treasures.difference(team_b_treasures)

print(unique_to_team_a)

This will print {"gold coin", "pearl"} because these treasures are only found by team A.

Sets are also useful for checking membership, just like dictionaries. You can use the in keyword to check if an item is in a set:

```
if "emerald" in team_b_treasures:

  print("Team B found an emerald!")

else:

  print("Team B did not find an emerald.")
```

This code checks if "emerald" is in the set of treasures found by team B and prints a message accordingly. Since "emerald" is in the set, it will print "Team B found an emerald!".

Both dictionaries and sets are potent tools that can help you organize and manage data efficiently in your programs. Dictionaries are perfect for storing and retrieving data using keys, making it easy to look up values quickly. They are ideal for tasks like storing contact information, managing inventories, and organizing complex data structures. Sets are great for keeping track of unique items and performing set operations, making them useful for tasks like managing collections of unique elements, checking for membership, and finding common or unique items between sets.

Understanding and using dictionaries and sets effectively can significantly enhance your ability to write efficient and organized programs. They provide powerful ways to store, retrieve, and manipulate data, allowing you to solve a wide range of problems easily. By practicing with dictionaries and sets, you will develop the skills needed to handle complex data structures and perform advanced data operations, making your programming experience more enjoyable and productive.

In conclusion, dictionaries and sets are essential tools in Python that help you manage and organize data efficiently. Dictionaries store data as key-value pairs, allowing you to look up values using keys quickly, add new entries, and update existing ones. They are perfect for tasks that require quick access to data and organization of complex information. Sets store collections of unique items, providing powerful ways to perform set operations and manage collections of unique elements. They are ideal for tasks that involve checking membership, finding common or unique items, and ensuring uniqueness in collections. You can write more efficient, organized, and powerful programs by understanding and using dictionaries and sets effectively. So, start practicing with dictionaries and sets today and discover how they can help you manage your data and build amazing projects!

CHAPTER V

Object-Oriented Programming Basics

What is Object-Oriented Programming?

Imagine you are creating a game with many different characters, each with unique abilities and characteristics. You need a way to organize all this information so you can easily manage and control the characters. This is where Object-Oriented Programming (OOP) comes in. OOP is a way of designing and writing programs that organize code around objects rather than actions. It makes programs easier to understand, reuse, and manage by modeling real-world things.

In OOP, everything is treated as an object. An object is a collection of data and functions that act on that data. Think of an object as a character in your game. Each character has attributes, like name, health, and strength, and actions they can perform, like attack or defend. In Python, you create objects using classes. A class is like a blueprint for creating objects. It defines the attributes and actions the objects created from the class will have.

Let's start by defining a simple class for a game character. A class is defined using the class keyword followed by the class name and a colon. Inside the class, you define functions (called methods) and variables (called attributes) that belong to the class. Here's an example of a basic class for a character:

```
class Character:

    def __init__(self, name, health, strength):
```

```python
        self.name = name

        self.health = health

        self.strength = strength


    def attack(self):

        print(f"{self.name} attacks with strength {self.strength}!")
```

In this example, we define a class called Character. The __init__ method is a special method called a constructor. It runs when you create a new object from the class. The __init__ method initializes the object's attributes. The self parameter refers to the object itself and allows you to access its attributes and methods. The attack method is a function that prints a message when the character attacks.

To create an object from a class, you call the class as if it were a function, passing the required arguments to the __init__ method. Here's how you create two characters and make them attack:

```python
character1 = Character("Aragorn", 100, 50)

character2 = Character("Legolas", 80, 70)


character1.attack()

character2.attack()
```

This code creates two objects, character1 and character2, from the Character class. It sets their names, health, and strength. When we call the attack method on each character, it prints the attack messages: "Aragorn attacks with strength 50!" and "Legolas attacks with strength 70!".

One of the main concepts in OOP is encapsulation. Encapsulation means bundling the data (attributes) and the methods (functions) that act on the data into a single unit, the object. This keeps the data safe from outside interference and misuse. In our example, the attributes name, health, and strength are encapsulated within the Character class. We access and modify them through the object's methods, ensuring controlled and safe interaction with the object's data.

Another important concept in OOP is inheritance. Inheritance allows a class to inherit attributes and methods from another class. This helps you create new classes that are similar to existing ones without rewriting the same code. For example, suppose we want to create a special type of character called a Wizard that has a magical power attribute. We can create a Wizard class that inherits from the Character class:

```python
class Wizard(Character):

    def __init__(self, name, health, strength, magic_power):

        super().__init__(name, health, strength)

        self.magic_power = magic_power


    def cast_spell(self):

            print(f"{self.name} casts a spell with power {self.magic_power}!")
```

In this example, the Wizard class inherits from the Character class using the syntax class Wizard(Character):. The __init__ method of the Wizard class calls the __init__ method of the Character class using super().__init__(name, health, strength) to initialize the inherited attributes. The Wizard class also adds a new attribute magic_power and a new method cast_spell.

Here's how you create a wizard and make them attack and cast a spell:

wizard = Wizard("Gandalf", 120, 30, 100)

wizard.attack()

wizard.cast_spell()

This code creates an object wizard from the Wizard class. When we call the attack method, it prints "Gandalf attacks with strength 30!". When we call the cast_spell method, it prints "Gandalf casts a spell with power 100!".

Inheritance allows you to create a hierarchy of classes that share common behavior. This makes your code more reusable and easier to maintain. You can create base classes with common attributes and methods and extend them with specialized classes that add new features.

Polymorphism is another key concept in OOP. Polymorphism allows different classes to be treated as if they are instances of the same class through a common interface. This means that objects of different classes can be used interchangeably if they share the same methods. For example, suppose we have another class called Archer that also inherits from the Character class and has a method called shoot_arrow:

```python
class Archer(Character):

    def __init__(self, name, health, strength, arrow_count):

        super().__init__(name, health, strength)

        self.arrow_count = arrow_count
```

```python
    def shoot_arrow(self):

        print(f"{self.name} shoots an arrow! {self.arrow_count} arrows left.")
```

Now, we can create a list of different characters and make them perform their unique actions:

```python
characters = [

    Wizard("Gandalf", 120, 30, 100),

    Archer("Legolas", 80, 70, 30)

]


for character in characters:

    character.attack()

    if isinstance(character, Wizard):

        character.cast_spell()

    elif isinstance(character, Archer):

        character.shoot_arrow()
```

In this example, we create a list of characters that includes both a wizard and an archer. We use a loop to go through each character and make them attack. We use the isinstance function to check the type of the character and call the appropriate method for each type. This demonstrates polymorphism because we treat objects of different classes (Wizard and Archer) as if they are instances of the same base class (Character) and call their unique methods based on their type. Encapsulation, inheritance, and polymorphism are the core principles of OOP that help you create flexible, reusable, and organized code. By modeling real-world things as objects with attributes and methods, you can build complex programs that are easier to understand and maintain. Let's look at a practical example of how OOP can be used in a simple game. Suppose we are creating a zoo simulation where we have different types of animals, and each animal can make a sound. We can create a base class Animal and extend it with specific animal classes like Lion, Elephant, and Monkey:

```python
class Animal:

    def __init__(self, name):

        self.name = name


    def make_sound(self):

        pass


class Lion(Animal):

    def make_sound(self):

        print(f"{self.name} roars!")


class Elephant(Animal):

    def make_sound(self):

        print(f"{self.name} trumpets!")


class Monkey(Animal):

    def make_sound(self):
```

```python
    print(f"{self.name} chatters!")
```

In this example, the Animal class is the base class with a method make_sound that does nothing (pass). The Lion, Elephant, and Monkey classes inherit from Animal and provide their own implementation of the make_sound method. This allows each animal to make a different sound.

Here's how we create different animals and make them sound:

```python
animals = [

  Lion("Simba"),

  Elephant("Dumbo"),

  Monkey("George")

]


for animal in animals:

  animal.make_sound()
```

This code creates a list of animals and makes each animal sound by calling their make_sound method. The output will be "Simba roars!", "Dumbo trumpets!", and "George chatters!". OOP helps you think about your programs regarding real-world objects, making it easier to design and build complex systems. By using classes and objects, you can create modular and reusable code that models the behavior and attributes of real things. This approach not only makes your code more organized but also makes it easier to extend and maintain.

In conclusion, Object-Oriented Programming is a powerful way of designing and writing programs by organizing code around objects. Objects are collections of data and functions that act on that data, and they are created using classes. The main principles of OOP are encapsulation, inheritance, and polymorphism. Encapsulation bundles data and methods into objects, inheritance allows classes to inherit attributes and methods from other classes, and polymorphism lets different classes be treated as instances of the same class through a common interface. By using OOP, you can create flexible, reusable, and organized code that models real-world things and makes your programs easier to understand and maintain. So start practicing with OOP today and discover how it can help you build amazing projects and solve complex problems!

Classes and Objects

Imagine you have a box of LEGO bricks and want to build different structures like houses, cars, and spaceships. Each structure you create is made up of different LEGO pieces put together in a specific way. In programming, classes and objects work similarly. A class is like a blueprint that defines how to build something, and an object is the actual thing you build using that blueprint. Classes and objects are fundamental concepts in Object-Oriented Programming (OOP), a way of organizing and writing code that makes creating complex and reusable programs easier.

A class in Python is a blueprint for creating objects. It defines the attributes (data) and methods (functions) that the objects created from the class will have. Think of a class as a template that describes what an object should look like and what it should be able to do. For example, if you were creating a class for a car, the attributes might include the car's color, brand, and speed, and the methods might include actions like start, stop, and accelerate.

To define a class in Python, you use the class keyword followed by the class name and a colon. Inside the class, you define the attributes and methods. Here's an example of a simple class called Car:

```python
class Car:

    def __init__(self, color, brand, speed):

        self.color = color

        self.brand = brand

        self.speed = speed


    def start(self):

        print(f"The {self.color} {self.brand} car starts!")


    def stop(self):

        print(f"The {self.color} {self.brand} car stops!")


    def accelerate(self):

        self.speed += 10

        print(f"The {self.color} {self.brand} car accelerates to {self.speed} mph!")
```

In this example, the Car class has an __init__ method, which is a special method called a constructor. The constructor is used to initialize the attributes of the class when an object is created. The self parameter refers to the object itself and allows you to access its attributes and methods. The Car class also has three methods: start, stop, and accelerate, which describe actions the car can perform.

To create an object from a class, you call the class as if it were a function, passing the required arguments to the __init__ method. Here's how you create two car objects and make them perform some actions:

```python
car1 = Car("red", "Toyota", 50)

car2 = Car("blue", "Honda", 60)


car1.start()

car1.accelerate()

car1.stop()


car2.start()

car2.accelerate()

car2.stop()
```

This code creates car1 and car2 objects from the Car class. It sets their color, brand, and speed attributes. When we call each car's start, accelerate, and stop methods, it prints messages like "The red Toyota car starts!" and "The blue Honda car accelerates to 70 mph!". One of the main benefits of using classes and objects is that they help you organize your code and make it more reusable. Instead of writing the same code multiple times, you can define a class once and create multiple objects from it. This makes your programs more efficient and easier to manage. For example, if you wanted to create a game with different types of characters, you could define a Character class and create objects for each character:

```python
class Character:

  def __init__(self, name, health, strength):
```

```python
        self.name = name

        self.health = health

        self.strength = strength


    def attack(self):

        print(f"{self.name} attacks with strength {self.strength}!")


    def heal(self):

        self.health += 10

        print(f"{self.name} heals and now has {self.health} health!")
```

You can then create different character objects and make them perform actions:

```python
character1 = Character("Aragorn", 100, 50)

character2 = Character("Legolas", 80, 70)


character1.attack()

character1.heal()


character2.attack()

character2.heal()
```

This code creates two character objects, character1 and character2, from the Character class. It sets their name, health, and strength attributes. When we call the attack and heal methods on each character, it prints messages like "Aragorn attacks with strength 50!" and "Legolas heals and now has 90 health!".

Another important concept in OOP is inheritance. Inheritance allows a class to inherit attributes and methods from another class. This helps you create new classes that are similar to existing ones without rewriting the same code. For example, if you wanted to create a special type of character called a Wizard that has a magical power attribute, you could create a Wizard class that inherits from the Character class:

```python
class Wizard(Character):

    def __init__(self, name, health, strength, magic_power):

        super().__init__(name, health, strength)

        self.magic_power = magic_power


    def cast_spell(self):

            print(f"{self.name} casts a spell with power {self.magic_power}!")
```

In this example, the Wizard class inherits from the Character class using the syntax class Wizard(Character):. The __init__ method of the Wizard class calls the __init__ method of the Character class using super().__init__(name, health, strength) to initialize the inherited attributes. The Wizard class also adds a new attribute magic_power and a new method cast_spell.

Here's how you create a wizard and make them perform actions:

```python
wizard = Wizard("Gandalf", 120, 30, 100)
```

wizard.attack()

wizard.heal()

wizard.cast_spell()

This code creates an object wizard from the Wizard class. When we call the attack, heal, and cast_spell methods on the wizard, it prints messages like "Gandalf attacks with strength 30!" and "Gandalf casts a spell with power 100!".

Inheritance allows you to create a hierarchy of classes that share common behavior. This makes your code more reusable and easier to maintain. You can create base classes with common attributes and methods and extend them with specialized classes that add new features.

Polymorphism is another key concept in OOP. Polymorphism allows different classes to be treated as if they are instances of the same class through a common interface. This means that objects of different classes can be used interchangeably if they share the same methods. For example, suppose we have another class called Archer that also inherits from the Character class and has a method called shoot_arrow:

class Archer(Character):

    def __init__(self, name, health, strength, arrow_count):

        super().__init__(name, health, strength)

        self.arrow_count = arrow_count

    def shoot_arrow(self):

        print(f"{self.name} shoots an arrow! {self.arrow_count} arrows left.")

Now, we can create a list of different characters and make them perform their unique actions:

```python
characters = [

    Wizard("Gandalf", 120, 30, 100),

    Archer("Legolas", 80, 70, 30)

]


for character in characters:

    character.attack()

    character.heal()

    if isinstance(character, Wizard):

        character.cast_spell()

    elif isinstance(character, Archer):

        character.shoot_arrow()
```

In this example, we create a list of characters that includes both a wizard and an archer. We use a loop to go through each character and make them perform actions. We use the isinstance function to check the type of the character and call the appropriate method for each type. This demonstrates polymorphism because we treat objects of different classes (Wizard and Archer) as if they are instances of the same base class (Character) and call their unique methods based on their type. Encapsulation, inheritance, and polymorphism are the core principles of OOP that help you create flexible, reusable, and organized code. By modeling real-world things as objects with attributes and methods, you can build complex programs that are easier to understand and maintain.

Let's look at another practical example of how a simple program can use classes and objects. Suppose you are creating a library system where you need to manage books and patrons. You can define a Book class and a Patron class:

```python
class Book:

    def __init__(self, title, author, available=True):

        self.title = title

        self.author = author

        self.available = available


    def check_out(self):

        if self.available:

            self.available = False

            print(f"{self.title} has been checked out.")

        else:

            print(f"{self.title} is already checked out.")


    def return_book(self):

        if not self.available:

            self.available = True

            print(f"{self.title} has been returned.")

        else:

            print(f"{self.title} was not checked out.")
```

```python
class Patron:

    def __init__(self, name):

        self.name = name

        self.checked_out_books = []


    def check_out_book(self, book):

        if book.available:

            book.check_out()

            self.checked_out_books.append(book)

        else:

            print(f"{book.title} is already checked out.")


    def return_book(self, book):

        if book in self.checked_out_books:

            book.return_book()

            self.checked_out_books.remove(book)

        else:

            print(f"{self.name} does not have {book.title} checked out.")
```

In this example, the Book class has attributes for the title, author, and availability of the book, and methods for checking out and returning the book. The Patron class has attributes for the patron's name, a list of checked-out books, and methods for checking out and returning books.

Here's how you create books and patrons and make them interact:

book1 = Book("The Hobbit", "J.R.R. Tolkien")

book2 = Book("Harry Potter and the Sorcerer's Stone", "J.K. Rowling")

patron = Patron("Alice")

patron.check_out_book(book1)

patron.check_out_book(book2)

patron.return_book(book1)

patron.return_book(book2)

This code creates two book objects and one patron object. The patron checks out and returns the books, and the program prints messages like "The Hobbit has been checked out." and "The Hobbit has been returned."

In conclusion, classes and objects are fundamental concepts in Object-Oriented Programming that help you create flexible, reusable, and organized code. A class is a blueprint that defines the attributes and methods of an object, while an object is an instance of a class that you create in your program. By using classes and objects, you can model real-world things, create complex programs, and make your code easier to understand and maintain. Encapsulation, inheritance, and polymorphism are the core principles of OOP that allow you to bundle data and methods, create hierarchies of classes, and treat different classes as if they are instances of the same class. So start practicing with classes and objects today and discover how they can help you build amazing projects and solve complex problems!

Inheritance: Extending Classes

Imagine you are playing a role-playing game where you can create different types of characters like warriors, wizards, and archers. Each character type has unique abilities but also shares common traits like health, strength, and the ability to attack. In programming, inheritance allows us to create classes that share common characteristics and also have their unique features. Inheritance helps us organize and reuse code, making our programs more efficient and easier to manage.

In Python, inheritance is a feature of Object-Oriented Programming (OOP) that allows a new class to inherit attributes and methods from an existing class. The existing class is called the parent or base class, and the new class is called the child or derived class. This means that the child class gets all the features of the parent class, and you can add new features or modify existing ones.

To understand inheritance, let's start with a simple example. Suppose we have a base class called Character that represents a generic character in our game. This class has attributes like name, health, and strength, and methods like attack and heal. Here's how we define the Character class:

```python
class Character:

    def __init__(self, name, health, strength):

        self.name = name

        self.health = health

        self.strength = strength

    def attack(self):
```

```python
    print(f"{self.name} attacks with strength {self.strength}!")

  def heal(self):

    self.health += 10

    print(f"{self.name} heals and now has {self.health} health!")
```

Now, let's say we want to create a special type of character called a Warrior that has an additional ability to defend. Instead of writing all the code for the Warrior class from scratch, we can make the Warrior class inherit from the Character class. This way, the Warrior class will have all the attributes and methods of the Character class, and we can add the defend ability. Here's how we define the Warrior class:

```python
class Warrior(Character):

  def __init__(self, name, health, strength, defense):

    super().__init__(name, health, strength)

    self.defense = defense

  def defend(self):

    print(f"{self.name} defends with a defense power of {self.defense}!")
```

In this example, the Warrior class inherits from the Character class using the syntax class Warrior(Character):. The __init__ method of the Warrior class calls the __init__ method of the Character class using super().__init__(name, health, strength) to initialize the inherited attributes. The Warrior class also adds a new attribute defense and a new method defend.

Now, let's create a warrior and make them perform some actions:

```python
warrior = Warrior("Aragorn", 100, 50, 20)


warrior.attack()

warrior.heal()

warrior.defend()
```

This code creates an object warrior from the Warrior class. When we call the attack, heal, and defend methods on the warrior, it prints messages like "Aragorn attacks with strength 50!" and "Aragorn defends with a defense power of 20!".

Inheritance allows us to create new classes that extend the functionality of existing ones without rewriting the same code. This makes our code more reusable and easier to maintain. We can create a hierarchy of classes that share common behavior, with each level of the hierarchy adding new features or modifying existing ones.

Let's add another type of character to our game. Suppose we want to create a Wizard class that inherits from the Character class and has an additional ability to cast spells. Here's how we define the Wizard class:

```python
class Wizard(Character):

    def __init__(self, name, health, strength, magic_power):

        super().__init__(name, health, strength)

        self.magic_power = magic_power


    def cast_spell(self):
```

```python
        print(f"{self.name} casts a spell with power {self.magic_power}!")
```

In this example, the Wizard class inherits from the Character class. The Wizard class has a new attribute magic_power and a new method cast_spell.

Here's how you create a wizard and make them perform some actions:

```python
wizard = Wizard("Gandalf", 120, 30, 100)


wizard.attack()

wizard.heal()

wizard.cast_spell()
```

This code creates an object wizard from the Wizard class. When we call the attack, heal, and cast_spell methods on the wizard, it prints messages like "Gandalf attacks with strength 30!" and "Gandalf casts a spell with power 100!".

Now let's create one more type of character called an Archer that has an additional ability to shoot arrows. Here's how we define the Archer class:

```python
class Archer(Character):

  def __init__(self, name, health, strength, arrow_count):

    super().__init__(name, health, strength)

    self.arrow_count = arrow_count


  def shoot_arrow(self):
    if self.arrow_count > 0:
      self.arrow_count -= 1
```

```python
        print(f"{self.name} shoots an arrow! {self.arrow_count} arrows left.")

    else:

        print(f"{self.name} has no arrows left!")
```

In this example, the Archer class inherits from the Character class. The Archer class has a new attribute arrow_count and a new method shoot_arrow.

Here's how you create an archer and make them perform some actions:

```python
archer = Archer("Legolas", 80, 70, 30)


archer.attack()

archer.heal()

archer.shoot_arrow()

archer.shoot_arrow()
```

This code creates an object archer from the Archer class. When we call the attack, heal, and shoot_arrow methods on the archer, it prints messages like "Legolas attacks with strength 70!" and "Legolas shoots an arrow! 29 arrows left.".

Using inheritance, we can create different types of characters that share common behavior and have unique abilities. This makes our code more modular and easier to understand. We can also add new character types to our game without changing the existing code.

Inheritance also allows us to use polymorphism, which means treating objects of different classes as if they are instances of the same class through a common interface. This allows us to write more flexible and reusable code.

For example, we can create a list of different characters and make them perform their unique actions using a loop:

```
characters = [

    Warrior("Aragorn", 100, 50, 20),

    Wizard("Gandalf", 120, 30, 100),

    Archer("Legolas", 80, 70, 30)

]


for character in characters:

    character.attack()
    character.heal()
    if isinstance(character, Warrior):
        character.defend()
    elif isinstance(character, Wizard):
        character.cast_spell()
    elif isinstance(character, Archer):
        character.shoot_arrow()
```

In this example, we create a list of characters that includes a warrior, a wizard, and an archer. We use a loop to go through each character and make them perform actions. We use the isinstance function to check the type of the character and call the appropriate method for each type. This demonstrates polymorphism because we treat objects of different classes (Warrior, Wizard, and Archer) as if they are instances of the same base class (Character) and call their unique methods based on their type.

Inheritance, polymorphism, and encapsulation are the core principles of OOP that help us create flexible, reusable, and organized code. By modeling real-world things as objects with attributes and methods, we can build complex programs that are easier to understand and maintain.

Let's look at another practical example of how inheritance can be used in a simple program. Suppose you are creating a library system where you need to manage books and patrons. You can define a base class Book and extend it with specialized classes for different types of books:

```python
class Book:

    def __init__(self, title, author):

        self.title = title
        self.author = author
        self.available = True

    def check_out(self):

        if self.available:
            self.available = False
            print(f"{self.title} has been checked out.")
        else:
            print(f"{self.title} is already checked out.")

    def return_book(self):

        if not self.available:
            self.available = True
            print(f"{self.title} has been returned.")
```

```python
    else:

        print(f"{self.title} was not checked out.")

class FictionBook(Book):

    def __init__(self, title, author, genre):

        super().__init__(title, author)

        self.genre = genre


    def describe(self):

        print(f"Fiction: {self.title} by {self.author}, Genre: {self.genre}")


class NonFictionBook(Book):

    def __init__(self, title, author, subject):

        super().__init__(title, author)

        self.subject = subject


    def describe(self):

        print(f"Non-Fiction: {self.title} by {self.author}, Subject: {self.subject}")
```

In this example, the Book class has attributes for the book's title and author, and methods for checking out and returning the book. The FictionBook and NonFictionBook classes inherit from the Book class and add new attributes for the genre and subject of the book, respectively. They also have a describe method that prints a description of the book.

Here's how you create books and describe them:

```python
book1 = FictionBook("The Hobbit", "J.R.R. Tolkien", "Fantasy")

book2 = NonFictionBook("A Brief History of Time", "Stephen Hawking", "Science")


book1.describe()

book2.describe()


book1.check_out()

book1.return_book()
```

This code creates a fiction book and a non-fiction book. The describe method prints descriptions like "Fiction: The Hobbit by J.R.R. Tolkien, Genre: Fantasy" and "Non-Fiction: A Brief History of Time by Stephen Hawking, Subject: Science". The check_out and return_book methods print messages like "The Hobbit has been checked out." and "The Hobbit has been returned.".

In conclusion, inheritance is a powerful feature of Object-Oriented Programming that allows us to create new classes that extend the functionality of existing ones. By inheriting attributes and methods from a parent class, we can create child classes with common behavior and unique features. Inheritance helps us organize and reuse code, making our programs more efficient and easier to manage. By practicing with inheritance, you can create flexible, reusable, and organized code that models real-world things and makes your programs easier to understand and maintain. So start exploring inheritance today and discover how it can help you build amazing projects and solve complex problems!

CHAPTER VI

File Handling and Basic Projects

Introduction to File Handling

Imagine you have a big box where you keep all your essential things like letters, drawings, and photos. Whenever you want to look at something or add something new, you open the box, find what you need, and then close the box when you're done. In programming, file handling works similarly. Files are like those boxes; they help us store, retrieve, and manage data outside our programs. Understanding how to handle files is an essential skill in programming because it allows us to save data, read data, and even share data with other programs.

Files come in many different types, but the most common types you'll work with are text files and binary files. Text files are used to store data that is readable by humans, such as documents or logs. Binary files are used to store data in a format that is readable by computers, such as images or executable programs. In Python, file handling is done using built-in functions and methods that make it easy to create, read, write, and delete files.

Let's start by learning how to open a file. To open a file in Python, you use the open function, which takes two arguments: the file name and the mode in which you want to open the file. The mode determines what you want to do with the file: read from it, write to it, or append data to it. Here's an example of how to open a file in read mode:

```python
file = open("example.txt", "r")
```

In this example, the file example.txt is opened in read mode, which means you can read the file's contents but not make any changes to it. The open function returns a file object, which you can use to perform various operations on the file. When you're done working with the file, you should always close it using the close method to free up system resources:

```python
file.close()
```

Reading from a file is one of the most common tasks you'll do with file handling. Once you have a file object, you can read its contents using methods like read, readline, and readlines. The read method reads the entire contents of the file and returns it as a single string:

```python
file = open("example.txt", "r")

content = file.read()

print(content)

file.close()
```

This code opens the file example.txt, reads its contents, and prints them to the screen. If the file contains the text "Hello, world!", that's what will be printed. The readline method reads one line at a time, which is useful if you want to process the file line by line:

```python
file = open("example.txt", "r")

line = file.readline()

while line:
    print(line.strip())
    line = file.readline()
file.close()
```

In this example, the file is read one line at a time inside a loop. The strip method removes any extra newline characters from the end of each line. The readlines method reads all the lines in the file and returns them as a list of strings:

```python
file = open("example.txt", "r")

lines = file.readlines()

for line in lines:

    print(line.strip())

file.close()
```

This code reads all the lines at once and then processes them using a for loop. Each line is printed after removing the newline characters.

Writing to a file is another common task. To write to a file, you need to open it in write mode ("w") or append mode ("a"). Write mode will create a new file if the file does not exist or overwrite the contents if it does. Append mode will add new data to the end of the file without removing the existing data. Here's how to open a file in write mode and write some text to it:

```python
file = open("example.txt", "w")

file.write("Hello, world!\n")

file.write("This is a new line.\n")

file.close()
```

This code creates a new file example.txt (or overwrites it if it already exists) and writes two lines of text to it. The write method does not automatically add newline characters, so you must include them in the strings you write.

To append data to an existing file, you open it in append mode:

```python
file = open("example.txt", "a")

file.write("This line will be added at the end.\n")

file.close()
```

This code adds a new line to the end of the file example.txt without affecting the existing content.

Sometimes, you must work with binary files, such as images or music files. Binary files contain data that is not meant to be read as text. To read or write binary files, you use the same open function but with modes "rb" for reading binary and "wb" for writing binary. Here's how to read a binary file:

```python
file = open("example.png", "rb")

content = file.read()

file.close()
```

This code opens an image file example.png in binary read mode and reads its contents. The data is stored in a variable as a bytes object, which is a sequence of bytes.

Writing to a binary file is similar:

```python
file = open("example_copy.png", "wb")
file.write(content)
file.close()
```

This code creates a new file example_copy.png and writes the binary data to it. In addition to reading and writing files, Python provides methods to handle other file operations, such as checking if a file exists, deleting a file, and getting information about a file. These operations are done using the os module, which provides a way to interact with the operating system. Here's how to check if a file exists and delete it:

```python
import os

if os.path.exists("example.txt"):

    os.remove("example.txt")

    print("File deleted.")

else:

    print("File does not exist.")
```

This code uses the os.path.exists method to check if example.txt exists. If it does, the os.remove method deletes the file.

You can also use the os module to get information about a file, such as its size and modification time:

```python
import os

if os.path.exists("example.txt"):

    file_info = os.stat("example.txt")

    print(f"Size: {file_info.st_size} bytes")

    print(f"Modified: {file_info.st_mtime}")

else:

    print("File does not exist.")
```

This code uses the os.stat method to get file information and prints the file size and modification time.

One of the useful features in Python for handling files is the with statement, which ensures that files are properly closed after they are used. The with statement creates a context in which the file is opened, and when the context is exited, the file is automatically closed. Here's an example of using the with statement to read a file:

```python
with open("example.txt", "r") as file:

    content = file.read()

    print(content)
```

In this code, the file example.txt is opened in read mode, and when the block inside the with statement is finished, the file is automatically closed. This makes the code cleaner and reduces the risk of leaving a file open accidentally.

You can also use the with statement to write to a file:

```python
with open("example.txt", "w") as file:

    file.write("Hello, world!\n")

    file.write("This is a new line.\n")
```

This code creates a new file example.txt and writes two lines of text to it. The file is automatically closed when the block is finished.

File handling is not just about reading and writing files; it also involves working with directories. Directories are folders that contain files and other directories. The os module provides methods to create, delete, and list directories. Here's how to create a new directory:

```python
import os


if not os.path.exists("new_directory"):
```

```python
    os.mkdir("new_directory")

    print("Directory created.")

else:

    print("Directory already exists.")
```

This code uses the os.mkdir method to create a new directory called new_directory. If the directory already exists, it prints a message indicating that.

To delete a directory, you use the os.rmdir method:

```python
import os

if os.path.exists("new_directory"):
    os.rmdir("new_directory")
    print("Directory deleted.")

else:

    print("Directory does not exist.")
```

This code deletes the new_directory if it exists.

You can also list the contents of a directory using the os.listdir method:

```python
import os

contents = os.listdir(".")
for item in contents:
    print(item)
```

This code lists all the files and directories in the current directory (represented by "."). Each item is printed on a new line.

Understanding file handling is essential for many programming tasks, such as data analysis, web development, and automation. Learning to read, write, and manage files allows you to create programs that interact with the real world, store data for later use, and share information with other programs.

Let's look at a practical file handling example in a simple project. Suppose you are creating a program to keep track of your favorite books. You want to store the list of books in a file so that you can add new books, view the list, and remove books. Here's how you can do this using file handling:

```python
import os


def add_book(title):
    with open("books.txt", "a") as file:
        file.write(f"{title}\n")
    print(f"Book '{title}' added.")


def view_books():
    if os.path.exists("books.txt"):
        with open("books.txt", "r") as file:
            books = file.readlines()
            if books:
                print("Your favorite books:")
                for book in books:
                    print(f"- {book.strip()}")
            else:
```

```python
            print("No books found.")
    else:
        print("No books found.")


def remove_book(title):
    if os.path.exists("books.txt"):
        with open("books.txt", "r") as file:
            books = file.readlines()
        with open("books.txt", "w") as file:
            for book in books:
                if book.strip() != title:
                    file.write(book)
        print(f"Book '{title}' removed.")
    else:
        print("No books found.")


while True:
    print("\n1. Add a book")
    print("2. View books")
    print("3. Remove a book")
    print("4. Exit")
    choice = input("Enter your choice: ")

    if choice == "1":
```

```python
        title = input("Enter the book title: ")
        add_book(title)
    elif choice == "2":
        view_books()
    elif choice == "3":
        title = input("Enter the book title to remove: ")
        remove_book(title)
    elif choice == "4":
        break
    else:
        print("Invalid choice. Please try again.")
```

This example has three main functions: add_book, view_books, and remove_book. The add_book function opens the books.txt file in append mode and adds a new book title to it. The view_books function opens the books.txt file in read mode and prints all the book titles. The remove_book function opens the books.txt file in read mode to read all the book titles, then writes back all the titles except the one to be removed.

The program runs in a loop, allowing users to add, view, remove books, or exit the program. This is a simple yet powerful example of how file handling can be used to create a helpful application that interacts with the real world.

In conclusion, file handling is a fundamental skill in programming that allows you to create, read, write, and manage files and directories. By learning how to handle files, you can store data for later use, process large amounts of data, and share information with other programs. Whether you are working with text files, binary files, or directories, Python provides a rich set of tools and methods to make file handling easy and efficient. So start practicing with file handling today and discover how it can help you build amazing projects and solve real-world problems!

Building Simple Projects

Imagine you are given a box of LEGO bricks and asked to build anything you want. The possibilities are endless: you can create a spaceship, a castle, or even a robot. Building simple projects in programming is very similar to this. You start with basic elements, such as variables, loops, and functions, and combine them to create something unique. These projects help you understand programming concepts better and give you the satisfaction of seeing your ideas come to life.

When you begin building simple projects in programming, it's essential to start with an idea that excites you. It could be a game, a tool to solve a problem, or something that just makes you happy. Starting with something you are passionate about makes learning fun and engaging. Let's explore some simple projects you can build, each designed to help you practice different programming skills.

One of the most straightforward projects you can start with is a number-guessing game. In this game, the computer randomly selects a number, and the player tries to guess it. The computer gives hints if the guess is too high or too low until the player guesses the correct number. This project helps you practice using variables, loops, conditionals, and random numbers. Here's how you can build it:

First, import the random module, which allows you to generate random numbers. Then, set up the game by choosing a random number between 1 and 100. You'll also need a loop that continues until the player guesses the correct number. Get the player's guess inside the loop and compare it to the chosen number. If the guess is too high or too low, print a hint. If the guess is correct, congratulate the player and end the loop. Here's the complete code:

import random

```python
def number_guessing_game():
    number_to_guess = random.randint(1, 100)
    guess = None

    print("Welcome to the Number Guessing Game!")
    print("I have chosen a number between 1 and 100. Can you guess it?")

    while guess != number_to_guess:
        guess = int(input("Enter your guess: "))

        if guess < number_to_guess:
            print("Too low! Try again.")
        elif guess > number_to_guess:
            print("Too high! Try again.")
        else:
            print("Congratulations! You guessed the correct number!")


number_guessing_game()
```

This project is a great way to practice basic programming concepts. You can expand it by adding more features, such as limiting the number of guesses or keeping track of how many guesses the player made.

Another fun project to build is a simple calculator. A calculator helps you perform basic arithmetic operations like addition, subtraction, multiplication, and division. This project helps you practice using functions and user input. Here's how you can build a simple calculator:

First, define functions for each arithmetic operation: add, subtract, multiply, and divide. Each function takes two numbers as parameters and returns the result. Then, set up the main part of the program to display a menu of options, get the user's choice, and perform the chosen operation. Here's the complete code:

```python
def add(a, b):

    return a + b


def subtract(a, b):

    return a - b


def multiply(a, b):

    return a * b


def divide(a, b):

    if b == 0:

        return "Error! Division by zero."

    else:

        return a / b


def calculator():

    print("Welcome to the Simple Calculator!")
```

```python
print("Select an operation:")
    print("1. Add")
    print("2. Subtract")
    print("3. Multiply")
    print("4. Divide")
    print("5. Exit")

    while True:
        choice = input("Enter your choice (1/2/3/4/5): ")

        if choice == "5":
            print("Goodbye!")
            break

        num1 = float(input("Enter the first number: "))
        num2 = float(input("Enter the second number: "))

        if choice == "1":
            print(f"The result is: {add(num1, num2)}")
        elif choice == "2":
            print(f"The result is: {subtract(num1, num2)}")
        elif choice == "3":
            print(f"The result is: {multiply(num1, num2)}")
        elif choice == "4":
```

```python
        print(f"The result is: {divide(num1, num2)}")

    else:

        print("Invalid choice! Please try again.")


calculator()
```

This project helps you understand how to use functions and user input to create a useful tool. You can enhance the calculator by adding more operations, such as exponentiation or square root, and improving the user interface.

If you enjoy games, creating a simple text-based adventure game can be a lot of fun. In this type of game, the player explores a fictional world by making choices that affect the story's outcome. This project helps you practice using variables, conditionals, loops, and functions. Here's how you can build a simple text adventure game:

First, create a storyline with different scenarios and choices. Define functions for each scenario, and use variables to keep track of the player's progress. Then, set up the main part of the program to start the game and guide the player through the choices. Here's an example of a simple text adventure game:

```python
def start_adventure():
    print("Welcome to the Text Adventure Game!")
    print("You find yourself in a dark forest. There are two paths ahead.")
    print("1. Take the left path.")
    print("2. Take the right path.")
    choice = input("Enter your choice (1/2): ")
```

```python
    if choice == "1":

        left_path()

    elif choice == "2":

        right_path()

    else:

        print("Invalid choice! Please try again.")

        start_adventure()

def left_path():

    print("You take the left path and encounter a friendly elf.")

    print("The elf offers you a magical potion.")

    print("1. Accept the potion.")

    print("2. Decline the potion.")

    choice = input("Enter your choice (1/2): ")

    if choice == "1":

        print("You drink the potion and feel a surge of strength!")

        print("Congratulations! You win!")

    elif choice == "2":

        print("You decline the potion and continue on your way.")
```

```python
        print("Unfortunately, you get lost and the adventure ends.")

    else:

        print("Invalid choice! Please try again.")

        left_path()


def right_path():

    print("You take the right path and encounter a sleeping dragon.")

    print("1. Try to sneak past the dragon.")

    print("2. Turn back and take the left path.")

    choice = input("Enter your choice (1/2): ")


    if choice == "1":

        print("You try to sneak past the dragon, but it wakes up!")

        print("The dragon breathes fire and you have to run away.")

        print("The adventure ends here.")

    elif choice == "2":

        left_path()

    else:

        print("Invalid choice! Please try again.")

        right_path()
```

start_adventure()

This project allows you to practice creating interactive stories and making decisions that affect the outcome. You can expand the game by adding more paths, scenarios, and characters to make it more complex and engaging.

Another simple but useful project is a to-do list application. This application helps you keep track of tasks you need to complete. It allows you to add, view, and remove tasks. This project enables you to practice using lists, functions, and user input. Here's how you can build a to-do list application:

First, define functions to add, view, and remove tasks. Use a list to store the tasks. Then, set up the main part of the program to display a menu of options, get the user's choice, and perform the chosen operation. Here's the complete code:

```python
tasks = []


def add_task():

    task = input("Enter a new task: ")

    tasks.append(task)

    print(f"Task '{task}' added.")


def view_tasks():

    if tasks:

        print("Your tasks:")

        for i, task in enumerate(tasks, start=1):

            print(f"{i}. {task}")
```

```python
    else:
        print("No tasks found.")


def remove_task():
  view_tasks()
  if tasks:
     task_number = int(input("Enter the number of the task to
remove: "))
      if 1 <= task_number <= len(tasks):
        removed_task = tasks.pop(task_number - 1)
        print(f"Task '{removed_task}' removed.")
      else:
        print("Invalid task number!")


def todo_list():
  print("Welcome to the To-Do List App!")
  while True:
     print("\n1. Add a task")
     print("2. View tasks")
     print("3. Remove a task")
     print("4. Exit")
     choice = input("Enter your choice (1/2/3/4): ")

     if choice == "1":
```

```python
        add_task()

    elif choice == "2":

        view_tasks()

    elif choice == "3":

        remove_task()

    elif choice == "4":

        print("Goodbye!")

        break

    else:

        print("Invalid choice! Please try again.")


todo_list()
```

This project helps you understand how to manage lists and create a simple user interface. You can enhance the to-do list application by adding features such as marking tasks as completed, saving tasks to a file, and loading tasks from a file.

Creating a quiz game is another exciting project. In a quiz game, players answer questions and receive points for correct answers. This project helps you practice using lists, loops, conditionals, and functions. Here's how you can build a simple quiz game:

First, create a list of questions and answers. Define a function to ask each question and check the answer. Use a loop to review the questions and track the player's score. Here's the complete code:

```python
questions = [
```

```python
    {"question": "What is the capital of France?", "answer": "Paris"},

    {"question": "What is 2 + 2?", "answer": "4"},

    {"question": "What is the color of the sky?", "answer": "blue"}

]


def ask_question(question):

    answer = input(question["question"] + " ")

    return answer.lower() == question["answer"].lower()


def quiz_game():

    print("Welcome to the Quiz Game!")

    score = 0

    for question in questions:

        if ask_question(question):

            print("Correct!")

            score += 1

        else:

            print("Wrong!")

    print(f"You scored {score} out of {len(questions)}.")

quiz_game()
```

This project allows you to practice creating and using dictionaries, working with lists, and creating interactive games. You can expand the quiz game by adding more questions, different types of questions (e.g., multiple choice), and keeping track of high scores.

Building simple projects is a great way to learn programming and apply what you've learned. It helps you practice using different programming concepts in a fun and meaningful way. Whether you are creating games, tools, or applications, starting with simple projects gives you the confidence to tackle more complex challenges in the future.

In conclusion, building simple projects is an exciting and effective way to learn programming. You can practice using programming concepts like variables, loops, functions, and conditionals by starting with ideas that interest you, such as games, tools, or interactive applications. Projects like a number guessing game, a simple calculator, a text adventure game, a to-do list application, and a quiz game help you understand how to organize your code, interact with users, and create useful and fun programs. As you gain more experience and confidence, you can take on more complex projects and continue to explore the endless possibilities of programming. So grab your box of programming "LEGO bricks" and start building something amazing today!

CHAPTER VII

Debugging and Troubleshooting

Common Errors in Python

Learning to program in Python is a fun and rewarding experience. However, like any skill, it comes with its challenges, one of which is dealing with errors. Errors in programming are normal and happen to everyone, even experienced programmers. Understanding common errors in Python and how to fix them is an essential part of becoming a good programmer. Let's explore some of the most common errors you might encounter while coding in Python and learn how to handle them.

One of the most frequent errors beginners face is the SyntaxError. This error occurs when Python encounters a line of code that it doesn't understand because it doesn't follow the correct syntax. Syntax errors are often caused by simple mistakes such as missing colons, parentheses, or indentation. For example, if you write an if statement without a colon at the end, you'll get a SyntaxError:

```
if 5 > 3

    print("Five is greater than three!")
```

To fix this error, you need to add a colon at the end of the if statement:

```
if 5 > 3:

    print("Five is greater than three!")
```

Another common error is the IndentationError. Python relies on indentation (spaces or tabs at the beginning of a line) to define the structure of the code, such as the blocks of code that belong to an if statement or a loop. If the indentation is not consistent, Python will raise an IndentationError. For example, the following code will cause an IndentationError because the second line is not indented correctly:

```
if 5 > 3:
print("Five is greater than three!")
```

To fix this error, you need to indent the second line properly:

```
if 5 > 3:

    print("Five is greater than three!")
```

A NameError occurs when you try to use a variable or function name that hasn't been defined yet. This can happen if you misspell a name or forget to define it before using it. For example, the following code will cause a NameError because the variable num is not defined:

```
print(num)
```

To fix this error, you need to define the variable before using it:

```
num = 5
print(num)
```

TypeError is another common error that occurs when you try to perform an operation on values of incompatible types. For example, if you try to add a number and a string, Python will raise a TypeError because these types cannot be added together:

```
num = 5
text = "Hello"
result = num + text
```

To fix this error, you must ensure the types are compatible. You can convert the number to a string or the string to a number, depending on what you want to achieve:

```
result = str(num) + text # Converts num to a string
# or
result = num + int(text) # Converts text to an integer (if text is a number)
```

A ValueError occurs when a function receives an argument of the right type but an inappropriate value. For example, if you try to convert a non-numeric string to an integer, Python will raise a ValueError:

```
num = int("Hello")
```

To fix this error, you must ensure the value is appropriate for the function. In this case, you need to provide a numeric string:

```
num = int("123")
```

IndexError happens when you try to access an element in a list or a string using an out-of-range index. For example, if you have a list with three elements and try to access the fourth element, you'll get an IndexError:

```python
numbers = [1, 2, 3]
print(numbers[3])
```

To fix this error, you must ensure the index is within the valid range. You can check the length of the list before accessing an element:

```python
if len(numbers) > 3:
    print(numbers[3])
```

A KeyError occurs when you try to access a key that does not exist in a dictionary. For example, if you have a dictionary with some keys and try to access a key that is not in the dictionary, you'll get a KeyError:

```python
ages = {"Alice": 25, "Bob": 30}
print(ages["Charlie"])
```

To fix this error, you can check if the key exists in the dictionary before accessing it:

```python
if "Charlie" in ages:
    print(ages["Charlie"])
else:
    print("Key not found")
```

AttributeError occurs when you try to access an attribute or method that does not exist for an object. For example, if you try to call a method that is not defined for a particular type of object, you'll get an AttributeError:

```python
text = "Hello"
```

```python
text.append(" World")
```

To fix this error, you must ensure the object has the attribute or method you're trying to access. In this case, you should use string concatenation instead of the append method:

```python
text = text + " World"
```

ZeroDivisionError occurs when you try to divide a number by zero, which is not allowed in mathematics. For example, the following code will cause a ZeroDivisionError:

```python
result = 10 / 0
```

To fix this error, you need to make sure the denominator is not zero before performing the division:

```python
denominator = 0
if denominator != 0:
    result = 10 / denominator
else:
    print("Cannot divide by zero")
```

FileNotFoundError occurs when you try to open a file that does not exist. For example, if you try to open a file that is not in the specified path, you'll get a FileNotFoundError:

```python
file = open("non_existent_file.txt", "r")
```

To fix this error, you must ensure the file exists and the path is correct before opening it. You can check if the file exists using the os.path.exists function:

```python
import os

if os.path.exists("non_existent_file.txt"):
```

```
    file = open("non_existent_file.txt", "r")

else:

    print("File not found")
```

Understanding and fixing these common errors is crucial to becoming a proficient Python programmer. Reading error messages carefully is essential, as they usually provide valuable information about what went wrong and where the error occurred. By practicing and debugging your code, you'll become better at identifying and solving errors, making your programming experience more enjoyable and productive.

Let's look at some additional tips for handling errors in Python. One useful technique is using try-except blocks to catch and handle exceptions. This allows your program to continue running even if an error occurs. Here's an example of how to use a try-except block to handle a potential error:

```
try:

    result = 10 / 0

except ZeroDivisionError:

    print("Cannot divide by zero")
```

In this code, the try block contains the code that might raise an exception. If a ZeroDivisionError occurs, the except block is executed, and a message is printed. You can also handle multiple exceptions by specifying multiple except blocks:

```
try:

    file = open("non_existent_file.txt", "r")

    result = 10 / 0

except FileNotFoundError:
```

```python
    print("File not found")
except ZeroDivisionError:
  print("Cannot divide by zero")
```

This code handles both FileNotFoundError and ZeroDivisionError, printing appropriate messages for each exception.

Another helpful technique is using the finally block, which runs code regardless of whether an exception occurred. This is useful for cleaning up resources, such as closing files:

```python
try:

  file = open("example.txt", "r")
  content = file.read()
except FileNotFoundError:
  print("File not found")

finally:

  file.close()
```

In this code, the finally block ensures that the file is closed, whether or not an exception was raised.

Understanding the different types of errors and how to handle them will make you a more confident and capable programmer. It's important to remember that encountering errors is a normal part of programming. Even experienced programmers make mistakes and encounter errors. The key is learning from these errors and using them to improve your coding skills.

In addition to the common errors we've discussed, there are some best practices you can follow to minimize errors and make your code more robust. One critical practice is writing clear and readable code. Using meaningful variable names, proper indentation, and comments can help you and others understand your code better and spot errors more easily.

Another best practice is testing your code thoroughly. Write test cases to check if your code behaves as expected in different scenarios. This can help you catch errors early and ensure your program works correctly. For example, you can write test cases for a function that adds two numbers:

```python
def add(a, b):

    return a + b


# Test cases

print(add(2, 3)) # Expected output: 5

print(add(-1, 1)) # Expected output: 0

print(add(0, 0)) # Expected output: 0
```

These test cases check if the add function returns the correct result for different inputs. You can verify that your function works as expected by running these tests.

Using version control systems like Git can also help you manage your code and track changes. Version control allows you to revert to previous code versions if something goes wrong and collaborate with others more effectively.

Lastly, seeking help from others and using online resources can be very beneficial. If you're stuck on an error, don't hesitate to ask for help from classmates, teachers, or online communities. Websites like Stack Overflow and GitHub are great places to find solutions and learn from other programmers.

In conclusion, common errors in Python, such as SyntaxError, IndentationError, NameError, TypeError, ValueError, IndexError, KeyError, AttributeError, ZeroDivisionError, and FileNotFoundError, are part of the learning process. Understanding these errors and knowing how to fix them is essential for becoming a proficient programmer. You can minimize errors and write more reliable code by reading error messages carefully, practicing debugging techniques, using try-except blocks, and following best practices. Remember that encountering errors is normal and an opportunity to learn and improve your programming skills. With patience and persistence, you'll become more confident in handling errors and enjoy the process of creating amazing projects with Python.

Debugging Techniques

Imagine you are a detective, solving a mystery to discover why something isn't working as it should. In programming, this process is called debugging. Debugging is like solving a puzzle where you identify and fix errors or bugs in your code. It can be challenging, but it can also be a fun and rewarding experience with the proper techniques. Learning effective debugging methods is essential for becoming a good programmer because it helps you understand your code better and ensures your programs run smoothly.

When you encounter a bug, the first step in debugging is to identify the problem. This often involves reading error messages carefully. Error messages provide valuable clues about what went wrong and where the error occurred. For example, if you see a SyntaxError, it means there is a problem with the structure of your code. The error message usually includes the line number where the problem was detected, which helps you locate the issue quickly. By reading and understanding error messages, you can often pinpoint the exact code line that needs fixing.

Once you have identified the problem, the next step is to understand why it happened. This involves examining the logic of your code and the data it is working with. One effective technique is to use print statements to display the values of variables at different points in your program. By printing the values of variables, you can see if they are what you expect them to be. For example, if your program is supposed to calculate the sum of two numbers but is giving the wrong result, you can add print statements to check the values of the numbers before and after the addition:

```python
a = 5

b = 3

print("Value of a:", a)

print("Value of b:", b)

sum = a + b

print("Sum:", sum)
```

In this code, the print statements show the values of a, b, and sum, helping you verify if the calculation is correct. If the output is not what you expect, you can trace the problem back to its source and fix it.

Another powerful debugging technique is using a debugger, a tool that allows you to step through your code line by line, inspect variables, and control the execution flow. Python comes with a built-in debugger called pdb. To use pdb, you can add the following line to your code where you want to start debugging:

```python
import pdb; pdb.set_trace()
```

When your program reaches this line, it will pause, and you can enter debugger commands to inspect and control the execution. For example, you can use the n command to execute the next line, the p command to print the value of a variable, and the c command to continue execution until the next breakpoint. By stepping through your code, you can see exactly how it executes and identify where things are going wrong.

Breakpoints are another helpful feature of debuggers. A breakpoint is a marker that you set in your code where you want the debugger to pause execution. This allows you to inspect the state of your program at specific points and identify issues. You can set breakpoints by clicking next to the line numbers in many Integrated Development Environments (IDEs) like PyCharm, VSCode, and Thonny. When the program runs and reaches a breakpoint, it will pause, and you can use the debugger to examine the program's state.

Sometimes, bugs are caused by incorrect assumptions about how your code should work. Writing unit tests can help you validate your assumptions and catch bugs early. Unit tests are small, automated tests that check if individual parts of your code work correctly. For example, if you have a function that calculates the area of a rectangle, you can write unit tests to verify that it returns the correct results for different inputs:

```python
def calculate_area(length, width):

  return length * width


def test_calculate_area():

  assert calculate_area(5, 3) == 15

  assert calculate_area(0, 5) == 0

  assert calculate_area(7, 2) == 14
```

test_calculate_area()

print("All tests passed!")

In this code, the test_calculate_area function contains several test cases that check if the calculate_area function returns the correct results. The assert statements verify that the function's output matches the expected values. If any test fails, the program will raise an AssertionError, indicating that there is a bug in the calculate_area function. By writing and running unit tests, you can catch bugs early and ensure your code behaves as expected.

Another helpful technique is code review, where you ask someone else to review your code. Fresh eyes can often spot mistakes that you might have missed. During a code review, the reviewer can provide feedback on your code's logic, readability, and potential issues. This collaborative process helps you improve your code quality and learn from others' perspectives.

Using version control systems like Git can also help with debugging. Version control allows you to track changes to your code and revert to previous versions if something goes wrong. For example, if you introduce a bug after making several changes, you can use Git to identify the specific change that caused the problem and revert to a working version. Git also provides features like branching and merging, which help you manage different versions of your code and collaborate with others more effectively.

Sometimes, bugs are caused by external factors, such as incorrect data or configuration settings. To debug these issues, you can use logging to record detailed information about your program's execution. Logging involves writing messages to a log file or console, which can help you track the program's behavior and identify issues. Python provides a built-in logging module that makes it easy to add logging to your code:

```python
import logging


logging.basicConfig(level=logging.DEBUG, format='%(asctime)s - %(levelname)s - %(message)s')


def calculate_area(length, width):

    logging.debug(f'Calculating area with length={length} and width={width}')

    area = length * width

    logging.debug(f'Calculated area: {area}')

    return area


calculate_area(5, 3)
```

In this code, the logging module is configured to display debug-level messages. The calculate_area function logs messages before and after calculating the area. These messages provide valuable information about the function's execution and can help you identify issues.

Handling exceptions is another important aspect of debugging. Exceptions are errors that occur during the execution of your program. By handling exceptions properly, you can prevent your program from crashing and provide useful error messages to the user. You can use try-except blocks to catch and handle exceptions:

```python
try:

    result = 10 / 0
```

except ZeroDivisionError:

  print("Cannot divide by zero")

In this code, the try block contains the code that might raise an exception. If a ZeroDivisionError occurs, the except block is executed, and a message is printed. By handling exceptions, you can make your program more robust and user-friendly.

Another effective technique for debugging is simplifying the problem. If you encounter a complex bug, try to isolate the part of your code that causes the issue. You can create a minimal, reproducible example that demonstrates the bug. By stripping away unnecessary code and focusing on the core problem, you can identify the issue more quickly and find a solution.

Refactoring your code can also help with debugging. Refactoring involves restructuring your code to make it cleaner and more readable without changing its behavior. By breaking down large functions into smaller, more manageable functions, you can make your code easier to understand and debug. For example, if you have a function that performs multiple tasks, you can refactor it into smaller functions, each responsible for a specific task:

def process_data(data):

  cleaned_data = clean_data(data)

  analyzed_data = analyze_data(cleaned_data)

  save_results(analyzed_data)

def clean_data(data):

  # Clean the data

  return cleaned_data

```python
def analyze_data(data):

    # Analyze the data

    return analyzed_data


def save_results(data):

    # Save the results
```

In this code, the process_data function is refactored into three smaller functions: clean_data, analyze_data, and save_results. This makes the code more modular and easier to debug.

Finally, developing a debugging mindset is crucial. Approach debugging with curiosity and persistence, treating it as an opportunity to learn and improve. Be patient and methodical, testing one change at a time and observing its effects. Keep track of what you have tried and the results, and don't be afraid to ask for help or search for solutions online. By developing a systematic approach to debugging, you can become more effective at identifying and fixing issues in your code.

In conclusion, debugging is an essential skill for every programmer. Understanding and using effective debugging techniques can help you identify and fix errors in your code, ensuring that your programs run smoothly. Reading error messages carefully, using print statements, employing debuggers, setting breakpoints, writing unit tests, conducting code reviews, using version control, adding logging, handling exceptions, simplifying problems, refactoring code, and developing a debugging mindset are all valuable techniques that can make debugging more manageable and successful. By practicing these techniques, you can become a more confident and capable programmer, ready to tackle any challenge that comes your way. Debugging is not just about fixing bugs; it's about learning, improving, and becoming better at creating amazing projects with code. So embrace the process, and enjoy the journey of becoming a skilled debugger.

Tips for Troubleshooting

Imagine you are trying to build a LEGO castle, but some pieces don't fit together, or parts of the structure keep falling apart. Troubleshooting your LEGO castle involves figuring out what went wrong and fixing it so your castle stands tall and looks fantastic. In Python programming, troubleshooting is similar. It's all about identifying and fixing what went wrong in your code to ensure your program runs smoothly. Here are some helpful tips for troubleshooting in Python, designed to make the process easier and more effective.

The first step in troubleshooting is understanding the error messages. When Python encounters an error in your code, it provides an error message that describes what went wrong. These messages might initially seem confusing, but they are like clues that can help you solve the problem. For example, if you see a SyntaxError, it means there is a mistake in how your code is written. The error message usually includes a line number showing where the problem occurred. By carefully reading the error message and looking at the specified line, you can often figure out what needs to be fixed.

Another important tip is to use print statements to understand what your code is doing. Print statements allow you to see the values of variables at different points in your program. For instance, if your program is not behaving as expected, you can add print statements to check the values of key variables. This can help you identify if a variable has an unexpected value, which might be causing the issue. By printing the values step by step, you can trace the flow of your program and understand where things are going wrong.

Using a debugger is another powerful way to troubleshoot your Python code. A debugger is a tool that allows you to run your code step by step, inspect variables, and control the execution flow. Python comes with a built-in debugger called pdb. To use pdb, you can add import pdb; pdb.set_trace() to your code where you want to start debugging. When your program runs and reaches this line, it will pause, allowing you to enter debugger commands. You can execute the next line of code with the n command, print the value of a variable with the p command, and continue execution until the next breakpoint with the c command. By using a debugger, you can see exactly how your code is executing and find the source of the problem.

Breaking your problem into smaller parts is another effective troubleshooting technique. If you have a large program and are unsure where the issue is, try isolating different sections of your code. For example, if you are working on a game and the scoring system is not working correctly, focus only on the part of your code that calculates the score. By simplifying the problem and testing smaller pieces of your code, you can identify where the issue lies and fix it more easily.

Writing tests for your code can also help you catch errors early and ensure that your program behaves as expected. Unit tests are small tests that check if individual parts of your code work correctly. For example, if you have a function that calculates the area of a rectangle, you can write tests to verify that it returns the correct result for different inputs. By running these tests, you can quickly identify if something is wrong with your function. Writing tests helps you catch bugs and makes your code more reliable.

Sometimes, looking at your code differently can help you spot errors. Taking a break and returning to your code later can give you a fresh perspective and make it easier to see what went wrong. Alternatively, you can ask someone else to review your code. Another person might notice something you missed and provide valuable feedback. Code reviews are a great way to learn from others and improve your troubleshooting skills.

Using version control systems like Git can also help with troubleshooting. Version control allows you to keep track of changes to your code and revert to previous versions if something goes wrong. For example, if you introduce a bug after making several changes, you can use Git to identify the specific change that caused the problem and revert to a working version. Version control also helps you collaborate with others and manage different versions of your code more effectively.

Understanding the importance of logging is another crucial tip for troubleshooting. Logging involves recording detailed information about your program's execution, which can help you track its behavior and identify issues. Python's built-in logging module makes adding logging to your code easy. By writing log messages, you can see what your program is doing at different points and find out where it is failing. Logging is especially useful for troubleshooting issues that occur in production environments, where you might not have direct access to the running program.

Handling exceptions properly is crucial for making your program more robust and easier to troubleshoot. Exceptions are errors that occur during the execution of your program. By using try-except blocks, you can catch and handle exceptions, preventing your program from crashing and providing useful error messages to the user. For example, if you are reading a file and the file does not exist, you can catch the FileNotFoundError exception and print a message to inform the user. Handling exceptions gracefully helps you manage errors more effectively and makes your program more user-friendly.

Finally, developing a systematic approach to troubleshooting is essential. Approach debugging with patience and persistence, testing one change at a time and observing its effects. Keep track of what you have tried and the results, and don't be afraid to ask for help or search for solutions online. By being systematic and organized, you can become more effective at identifying and fixing issues in your code.

In conclusion, troubleshooting in Python is like solving a puzzle or playing detective. You can become a more confident and capable programmer by understanding error messages, using print statements, employing a debugger, breaking problems into smaller parts, writing tests, seeking fresh perspectives, using version control, logging, handling exceptions, and developing a systematic approach. Troubleshooting is an essential skill that helps you understand your code better and ensures your programs run smoothly. With practice and persistence, you can master the art of troubleshooting and enjoy the process of creating unique projects with Python.

CONCLUSION

As we conclude this book on Python programming for kids, I hope you feel excited and empowered to continue your journey in the world of coding. You've learned about fundamental concepts like variables, loops, and functions, and explored more advanced topics such as file handling, debugging, and object-oriented programming. By building simple projects, troubleshooting common errors, and mastering debugging techniques, you've gained the skills needed to create your own unique programs.

Remember, programming is not just about writing code; it's about solving problems, thinking creatively, and continually learning. Every error is an opportunity to improve, and every project is a chance to apply what you've learned in new and exciting ways. Keep experimenting, ask questions, and don't be afraid to make mistakes. With persistence and curiosity, you'll continue to grow as a programmer.

Thank you for embarking on this journey with me. Whether you're building games, creating tools, or exploring new ideas, I hope this book has sparked your passion for Python and shown you the endless possibilities of what you can achieve with code. Happy coding!

Thank you for buying and reading/ listening to our book. If you found this book useful/ helpful please take a few minutes and leave a review on the platform where you purchased our book. Your feedback matters greatly to us.